Funky Fungi

OTHER TITLES IN THE
YOUNG NATURALISTS SERIES

Amazing Amphibians: 30 Activities and Obeservations for
Exploring Frogs, Toads, Salamanders, and More

Awesome Snake Science! 40 Activities
for Learning About Snakes

Birdology: 30 Activities and Observations
for Exploring the World of Birds

Insectigations: 40 Hands-on Activities
to Explore the Insect World

Plantology: 30 Activities and Observations
for Exploring the World of Plants

Treecology: 30 Activities and Observations for
Exploring the World of Trees and Forests

Funky Fungi

30 Activities for Exploring Molds, Mushrooms, Lichens, and More

ALISHA GABRIEL and SUE HEAVENRICH

CHICAGO REVIEW PRESS

Published by Chicago Review Press Incorporated
814 North Franklin Street
Chicago, Illinois 60610
ISBN 978-1-64160-577-9

Library of Congress Control Number: 2022933784

Cover and interior design: Sarah Olson
Cover photographs: (front cover) Beefsteak fungus,
Marjolein Tschur/Wikimedia Commons; Bristly beard tree
moss, vaitekune/stock.adobe.com; Mushrooms in the wild,
courtesy of Terrie Crance; Octopus stinkhorn, Bernard
Spragg/Wikimedia Commons; Golden chanterelle, Ron
Pastorino/Mushroom Observer; Morels, Drew Heath/
Wikimedia Commons; Orange peel fungus, Aiwok/
Wikimedia Commons; (back cover) Assorted mushrooms,
Alexander Potapov/stock.adobe.com
Illustrations: Jim Spence

Printed in the United States of America
5 4 3 2 1

This book is dedicated to mycologists, conservationists, and citizen scientists of all ages who are passionate about the fungi all around us.

To Noel, who never stopped encouraging me.
—Alisha Gabriel

To Mom and Dad, who supported and encouraged my curiosity.
—Sue Heavenrich

Contents

Introduction viii

1. Is There a Fungus Among Us? 1

Try This! Make a FUNgus Journal 4

Try This! Put Together an Explorer's Pack 7

Look For: Name That Fungus 11

Try This! Dissect a Mushroom 12

2. Sorting Out the Fungi 15

Look For: Go on a Fungal Foray 18

Try This! Make a Spore Print 21

Try This! Build a Simple Microscope 25

Try This! Design Your Own Fungus 27

3. Fungi Hold the World Together 31

Try This! What Happens If You Don't Rake the Grass? 34

Try This! Fold a Fungus Bookmark. 38

Look For: Lichen-Looking Expedition 41

4. Fungi as Food 45

Try This! What's for Sale? 48

Try This! Make Your Own Yeast 51

Look For: Identifying Wild Mushrooms 54

Try This! Plan Your Own Fungi Fest. 55

5. When Fungi Go Bad .57

Taste It: Cook a Corn Mushroom Taco. 60

Try This! Make Your Own Fungus-Fighting Mix 62

Try This! Mushroom Stamp Art 64

Look For: We're Going on a Zombie Hunt. 67

6. The Fungal Pharmacy 69

Try This! Design a Postage Stamp 71

Try This! Do Mushrooms Absorb Water? 74

Try This! Lobby for a State Fungus 78

Try This! Follow a Fungus Friend 79

7. Putting Fungi to Work 81

Try This! Grow a Mold Garden 83

Try This! Write a Haiku 85

Try This! Bundle Dye with Fungi 90

8. The Future of Fungi 93

Try This! Adopt an Endangered Fungus 95

Try This! Send a Soil Sample 99

Try This! Make Paper Out of Fungi 100

Try This! Make Compost in a Soda Bottle 102

Glossary 105

Online Resources 107

Teacher's Guide 108

Notes 110

Bibliography 111

Index 112

Introduction

When you bite into a mushroom-topped pizza, you're eating a fungus. And that fuzzy **mold** splotched on the cheese at the back of the fridge? That's a fungus too. From thick, shelf-like brackets growing on trees to hard, bumpy **lichens** covering boulders, there are fungi all around us. So many that, if you scooped a single teaspoon (4.2g) of soil from your garden, there would be several yards of fungal filaments. Like most of the fungi on our planet, they are too small to see without magnification.

Several young specimens of tinder fungus (*Fomes fomentarius*) growing on a tree. *Reinhold Möller/Wikimedia Commons*

If you ask a friend what a fungus is, chances are they'll mention **mushrooms**. Mushrooms are actually the **fruiting** bodies of fungi, and they come in a fascinating array of bright corals, darkly colored brains, and spotted umbrellas. Fungi are not only beautiful, they are also important to everything living around them: people, plants, and animals.

Fungi are nature's **decomposers**, turning fallen leaves, branches, and trees into **nutrients** for the next generation of forest seedlings. They also form partnerships with plants, helping move nutrients to roots. They provide food for deer, squirrels, and rabbits as well as slugs and insects. And if some fungi cause itchy feet and human diseases, others are used to cure disease. Crime scene investigators use fungi to help determine who-done-it, and clean-up crews depend on fungi to clear toxic spills.

Fungi have inhabited the Earth for nearly a billion years and are a diverse group. There are more than 140,000 named species and scientists are discovering new ones every year. By comparison, there are around 6,500 species of mammals. Researchers estimate that most of the world's fungi have yet to be discovered

Clathrus archeri, commonly called octopus stinkhorn, photographed in Christchurch, New Zealand. *Bernard Spragg. NZ/Wikimedia Commons*

and that the total number of fungi might be close to 3.5 million species. In 2017 scientists described an orange salt-tolerant mushroom collected in the Andes mountain range in Chile. A couple years later, scientists found two new species of fungi in a melting glacier in the Canadian arctic. Imagine growing in below-freezing temperatures! Brrrrr!

Like animals and plants, fungi are threatened by **habitat** loss, climate change, pollution, and over-harvesting. Even simple acts, such as clearing dead wood, can affect fungi that play a critical role in the forest habitat. Conservationists and scientists are working together to protect **endangered** fungi and their landscapes before it is too late.

This book isn't a field guide. It is more of a jumping-off point for explorations into the hidden kingdom. We encourage you to create an explorer's notebook, pack up your kit, and discover the fascinating, funky fungi where you live. We'll even share some ways you can get involved as a citizen scientist and conservationist.

IMPORTANT!

Never eat a fungus that you find—it could be poisonous. Fungi can be difficult to identify, even for seasoned explorers, so it's best not to touch unknown fungi with your bare hands. If you find a fungus and want to use it for an experiment, be careful when handling it. **Don't smell fungi either.** You could breathe in thousands of microscopic **spores** and become ill. And remember to wash your hands after dealing with fungi.

Fungus-finding is fun, but make sure you tell an adult where you are going. If you plan to go farther than your backyard, you should ask a parent or adult to accompany you.

During the day, the poisonous, bioluminescent jack-o-lantern fungus (*Omphalotus olearius*) can be mistaken for edible mushrooms. *Courtesy of Liam McGranaghan*

1

Is There a Fungus Among Us?

No matter where you are at this very minute, there is a good chance that there's a fungus or two nearby. That's because fungi (plural of fungus) live all around us. They live in the air, in our homes, in soil and sand, on rocks, on plants and animals, in the deepest part of the ocean, and even on your body. While some form mushrooms, most fungi are so small you can't see them without using a microscope.

Mycologists, scientists who study fungi, have described and named over 140,000 species

Mycena leaiana var. australis. Picture taken in Mount Field National Park, Tasmania, **Australia.** *JJ Harrison/Wikimedia Commons*

of mushrooms, molds, and yeasts. They have found fungi living in hot springs, growing in salty soil in the Chilean Andes, thriving on radioactivity inside the Chernobyl nuclear power plant in Ukraine, and surviving in the below-freezing temperatures of Arctic glaciers.

Fungus Fundamentals

More than 2,300 years ago, Aristotle divided living things into two major groups: plants and animals. Because mushrooms were plantlike, they were included in the group of "lower plants" along with liverworts and mosse At the time, this probably made sense. After all, when you pull a mushroom gently from the soil, you'll notice thin root-like threads attached to the bottom. And even though they don't have flowers, mushrooms do produce spores, which resemble very small seeds.

The first person to discover and prove that mushrooms grow from spores was Pier Antonio Micheli, a Catholic priest and famous Italian botanist. In the 1720s he sliced a melon and placed spores from a fungus on the melon slices. The spores germinated and eventually grew fruiting bodies that were identical to the ones he had taken the spores from. He proved that fungi did not grow from "spontaneous generation," which was the accepted theory until then.

Today, Micheli is known as the "father of mycology" because he was the first person to experiment with fungi. He named the genus *Aspergillus* after an aspergillum, a tool that priests use to sprinkle holy water. The spores of *Aspergillus* fungi form thin, threadlike **hyphae** (HY-fee) in a round, pom-pom shape.

In the years after Micheli's discoveries, scientists began noticing important differences between plants and fungi. The most obvious one: plants make their own food. Plants contain chlorophyll, a pigment that enables them to use sunlight so they can convert carbon dioxide into sugar. Even liverworts, plants that have no true roots, stems, or leaves, can make their own food using **photosynthesis.** But not fungi. Hungry fungi obtain their energy by dissolving their food—plant or animal matter, even bacteria and other fungi—outside their bodies. Then they absorb the nutrients they need.

In 1957, ecologist Robert Whittaker proposed classifying organisms into three kingdoms based on how they fit into the food chain. Producers would include plants, organisms that made their own food. Consumers would include all

ALL IN GOOD FUN

How you pronounce fungi depends on where you live. In the United States, it sounds like FUN-guy. As in: "Why was the mushroom invited to the party? Because he's a fun guy!" Across the pond—in the United Kingdom—they pronounce it differently. The end of the word makes a long E sound, making it FUN-gee.

Fungus found while walking at a park.
Courtesy of Gerri Wiley

FROM THE FUNGUS FILES:
The Humongous Fungus (*Armillaria ostoyae*)

You might think the largest living organism on Earth is a blue whale, but it's really a fungus. It might even be the oldest living organism. Scientists think *Armillaria ostoyae*, nicknamed the "humongous fungus," could be as many as 8,650 years old. This fungus lives in Oregon's Malheur National Forest and is so big that it covers 3.75 square miles (10 sq km). You could fit 1,815 American football fields into that area! And it's still growing—about one to three feet outward each year. Most of the time it doesn't look like much: a thin white mat growing under the bark of trees and down among the roots. If you scraped it all into one pile, scientists estimate it would weigh more than

200 gray whales. In the fall, the humongous fungus produces amber-colored fruiting bodies that people call honey mushrooms.

The fruiting bodies of *Armillaria ostoyae* are often the only evidence that people see of this huge fungus. *Alan Rockefeller/Mushroom Observer*

FUNGUS-OLOGY?

The study of animals is called zoology. The study of bacteria is called bacteriology. So what's the study of fungi called? In the 1800s people referred to the study of mushrooms as fungology. That's because the word *fungus* means mushroom in Latin. Today, **mycology** is the recognized term for the study of fungi. The prefix "myco" comes from the Greek word *mykes*, meaning mushroom.

Statue of Pier Antonio Micheli outside the Uffizi Gallery in Florence, Italy.
Sailko/Wikimedia Commons

animals. Decomposers would include fungi and bacteria, organisms that break down dead and decaying organisms. Twelve years later, Whittaker advocated a more detailed five-kingdom system for classification of life, an idea the scientific community eventually embraced. That's when kingdom Fungi officially gained its individual status.

Scientists are still discussing how best to classify organisms. Though many do not agree on how many kingdoms there should be, they do agree that fungi deserve their own.

Advances in science and technology from the 1970s through today have allowed researchers to compare the genes of living

Make a FUNgus Journal

Like other scientists, you'll need a notebook to collect data from experiments and draw pictures of the fungi you meet as you explore. Here's how to make your own FUNgus journal using materials found around the house.

MATERIALS

- 🍄 Empty cereal box
- 🍄 Scissors
- 🍄 Ruler
- 🍄 Wrapping paper, fabric, magazines, old maps
- 🍄 School glue
- 🍄 Paintbrush
- 🍄 10–12 sheets of plain or graph paper, 8.5 x 11 inches (22 x 28 cm)
- 🍄 Adult helper
- 🍄 Needle with large eye
- 🍄 Sharp nail (or awl)
- 🍄 24 inches (61 cm) of yarn, string, or embroidery floss

1. Cut out a 9-inch by 11½-inch (23 x 29 cm) rectangle from a cereal box.

2. Fold the cereal box in half like a book, with the plain side on the inside. Use a ruler to help press the crease.

3. Cut or tear wrapping paper, fabric, magazines, or old maps to make a journal cover. Brush glue on the colored side of the cereal box cardboard and press paper or fabric on it. Rub the paper from the center to the edges to smooth out bubbles. Make sure that about ½ inch (a bit more then 1 cm) or so of the paper or fabric extends past the edge of the cardboard.

4. Once the glue is dry, turn the cover over. Cut the edges of paper or fabric at the corners as shown.

5. Fold and glue the paper over the edges.

6. Fold the sheets of paper in half like a book. Open them up and mark three points along the fold: one about 2 inches (5 cm) from the top edge, one in the middle, and one about 2 inches (5 cm) from the bottom edge. With an adult helper, use the needle to poke holes where you marked. Then use the nail to make the holes bigger.

7. Center the papers along the fold of the cardboard cover and mark where the holes are. Use the needle and nail to poke holes through the cardboard.

8. Thread the yarn or string through your needle, pulling through 3–4 inches (8–10 cm). Line up the paper and cover so the holes meet.

9. Push the needle through the center hole of the paper and through the cover, leaving a tail of 4–6 inches (10–15 cm).

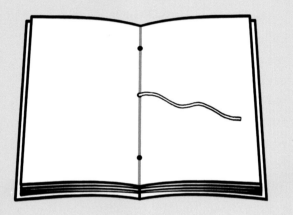

10. From the outside, push the needle through the top hole of the cover and through the paper.

11. From the inside, push the needle through the bottom hole of the paper and through the cover.

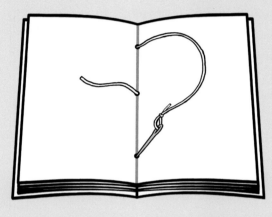

12. From the outside, push the needle through the center hole. When it comes through the paper, bring the needle up on the other side of the yarn from the original tail. Tie the yarn in a knot and snip off long ends.

things, right down to their **molecules**. They have found that fungi are eukaryotic organisms, which means they have a nucleus within every cell, just like plant and animal cells. Plant and fungus cells have cell walls, but animal cells don't. When researchers took a closer look, they noticed that the cell walls in plants contain cellulose, but the cell walls in fungi contain **chitin** (KY-tin). Chitin is the same substance that makes up the exoskeletons of insects and the shells of lobsters and crabs.

DNA studies also showed that fungi are more closely related to animals than they are to plants. Scientists speculate that animals and fungi share a common ancestor after plants branched off. This could explain why fungal infections, such as athlete's foot, are so difficult to treat.

The Nuts and Bolts of Sorting Fungi

Imagine someone gives you a bucket of fasteners and asks you to sort them. When you spread them out, you see there are nuts and bolts, screws and washers, and even a few nails. You begin putting similar things in a pile: nuts over here, screws over there. Later, as you examine the screws, you notice some are flat-topped and some are round-topped, so you divide those into different piles. Then you notice that some have a single line across the head and others have an X, some are long and some are short.

Taxonomists—scientists who describe and classify organisms—do something similar. In the 1700s, a Swedish scientist named Carl Linnaeus started grouping living things by what they had in common. He also decided to give each organism a two-word Latin name. This naming of species is called **binomial nomenclature**. The first word tells us the genus, and the second tells us the species name. For example, humans are called *Homo sapiens. Homo* is from Latin and means "human being" and *sapiens* means "wise." A recently discovered orange fungus was named after a cartoon character because it smells fruity, looks like a sea sponge, and bounces back to its original shape after being squeezed. Its scientific name is *Spongiforma squarepantsii.*

Scientific names are important for distinguishing one species from another.

Many people use common names for animals, trees, flowers, and fungi, but sometimes that gets confusing. For example, when someone in New York says there's an Indian paintbrush growing in their yard, they could mean *Castilleja coccinea*, a plant with red bracts that look like tubular flowers. Or they could be referring to *Hieracium aurantiacum*, a small, orange, dandelion-like flower also known as hawkweed.

Sometimes several similar species are called by the same name, such as bluebonnets. The flowers, which grow on spikes, each look like a bonnet worn by pioneer women of the American West. Similar confusion happens with fungi as well. Many of the *Amanita* mushrooms look similar, but some are poisonous and some are not. When working with fungi, researchers need to know exactly which species they have.

Fungal Anatomy

The parts we call mushrooms are the spore-producing fruiting bodies of fungi. Some look like umbrellas, with **stalks** and **caps.** Others might have flat tops or form round puffballs. Pitcher fungi look like miniature vases, whereas a lion's mane fungus clumps together with strands that hang down and

FROM THE FUNGUS FILES:
Jelly Ear Fungus from the Genus *Auricularia*

Talk softly in the forest, because the trees have ears. These fungi, called jelly ears, wood ears, or tree ears, appear on trees after it rains. Some are fan-shaped and resemble ears, while others are oval or even cup-shaped. Their reddish-brown surface

feels a bit rubbery or gelatinous. Several species are edible, and some are farmed. They contain an anticoagulant compound (material that reduces blood clotting) and are used in Chinese medicine.

Some trees have ears—or at least jelly ear fungi (*Auricularia auricula-judae*). *Josh Milburn/ Mushroom Observer*

Put Together an Explorer's Pack

When you go out to explore the world of fungi, you'll want to carry a few tools along with your FUNgus Journal. Make an Explorer's Pack to take along! Use an old school backpack or messenger bag. Your Explorer's Pack doesn't have to be pretty—just sturdy. Load it up with things on this list, and you'll be ready to head off to explore.

Some things to put in your Explorer's Pack:

- Your FUNgus Journal and a pen or pencil, so you can jot down notes about what you find.
- Colored pencils or a watercolor set with a brush, for sketching mushrooms and other fungi.
- A digital camera or a smartphone. You can upload images from a smartphone to a nature app to help identify what you've found.
- A hand lens or magnifying glass, so you can look at details.

- A plastic ruler, because size matters when you're trying to figure out what you've found.
- A trowel or other digging tool, if you want to take a sample home to study.
- A pocket knife or plastic picnic knife, to gently cut specimens for study.
- Small paper bags or wax paper bags, to carry home specimens for further study.
- A sharpie or marker, to write down where you found a specimen and other notes right on the bag.
- A field guide to mushrooms (see field guides listed on page 111, or search for a guide specific to your state or region. You can also download a free copy of the *USDA Field Guide to Common Macrofungi in Eastern Forests and Their Ecosystem Functions* at www.nrs.fs.fed .us/pubs/38089).
- A paper mask, to protect you from breathing in spores.

Toss in a bottle of water and a snack and you're set for a couple hours of exploring. Remember to put on sunscreen and spray on some insect repellent to discourage ticks.

Yellow Fly Agaric (*Amanita muscaria* var. *formosa*) is common in the northeast United States. *Sue Heavenrich/Author photo*

thin to a point. Some fungi, like purple coral fungi and stinkhorns, seem like they belong under the sea instead of in the woods. Stinkhorns look egg-like until the sides open. Then they resemble an octopus's tentacles!

The fruiting bodies are the part of the fungus we see. The major part of a fungus is a cobweb of thin threads growing beneath the soil or spreading through leaf litter and under bark. Imagine what you would see if fruit trees grew underground. You'd never see their trunks, branches, twigs, and leaves. The only time you would

notice them would be when they fruited—and then you'd only see the apples, peaches, pears, or plums poking up through the soil.

Most fungi don't produce fruiting bodies. Not only that, most are so small you'd need a microscope to see them, so you might not realize they're living all around us. You probably don't notice molds until they've grown a colony on a piece of bread or fruit, or in the corner of your shower. And baker's yeast (*Saccharomyces cerevisiae*) is a single-celled fungus so tiny that 3,000 could easily fit on the period at end of this sentence.

A fungus begins life as a tiny spore. To germinate, the spore needs organic matter such as fallen leaves, downed branches, or a pizza crust. It also needs moisture. First, the spore sends out rootlike threads called hyphae. They push through soil and leaf litter and across objects to reach food. Hyphae are similar to a plant's roots, but they are much, much thinner. If you rub a strand of hair through your fingers, you'll notice how thin and fragile it feels. A single hypha is about one-tenth the thickness of a single human hair. When hyphae clump together, they might remind you of cobweb threads.

Hyphae grow toward a food source and, when they reach it, secrete **enzymes**

to digest it. The enzymes break down the plant or animal matter into simple sugars and **amino acids**, which the hyphae absorb. Those nutrients provide energy for the fungus to keep growing. When hyphae no longer sense food, they stop growing to conserve their energy.

As soon as hyphae detect another food source, they begin growing again, branching out in a circular pattern. This forms a thicker, mat-like network called a **mycelium** (my-SEE-lee-um). Now, imagine you get gum in your hair. The strands of your hair are stuck to the gum and point every which way. The mycelium of some fungi is a little like this. Instead of gum, the part that's getting bigger and thicker is forming a fruiting body in order to reproduce. Below the surface, there's often an elaborate, hidden network of mycelia.

No Fruit? No Problem

Molds don't produce fruiting bodies, but they do make spores. Most molds form transparent hyphae which, over time, grow into a tiny fuzzy-looking mycelium. That's the grayish-white fuzz you see on a strawberry, or the dusty white and green powder on the peel of an orange. The fact that you can see it means that the mold has reproduced over and over and formed a colony. Molds reproduce by forming millions of microscopic spores at the ends of their hyphae. Once released into the air, mold spores drift until they land on a surface. If conditions are right, they begin growing. If not, a mold spore can remain dormant until the right conditions develop.

Some molds are cute and fuzzy, but others can cause problems. For people who are allergic to them, molds cause respiratory (breathing) trouble. Not all molds are harmful to humans, and many play an important role in the **ecosystem**. People cultivate certain molds to make soy sauce and blue cheese, and the antibiotic penicillin originated from the mold *Penicillium rubens*.

Spores Galore

Molds and fruiting bodies produce spores, much like a plant produces seeds. The biggest difference? Fungal spores are microscopic, and a single fungus can produce trillions of spores.

Oval, round, long, skinny, smooth, spiky, striped, hard, soft—these are just a few of the shapes and characteristics that spores can take. Some spores are so light that they can ride on wind currents. Others travel by sticking on people's clothing or animal fur. Some spores travel by water. Others are eaten and pooped out by wildlife. Many spores have evolved to withstand harsh conditions.

Giant puffball mushrooms release their spores with a powerful whoosh. If you tap one with a stick, it sends trillions

Hyphae growing on wood.
Aurélien Adoue/Flickr

Mycelium growing on rye bread.
Sue Heavenrich/Author Photo

of spores into the air in a puff of smoke. Texas star mushrooms burst open with a hiss to release their spores, and bird's nest fungi rely on raindrops to splash their spores into the world. Stinkhorns attract flies for spore dispersal. The mushrooms produce a stinky brown slime that flies love. As flies walk around on the sticky goo, they pick up spores, and then fly away, carrying the spores to new places.

BUDDING BUDDIES

Almost all fungi reproduce by forming spores, but not yeasts. Yeasts are single-cell microorganisms that reproduce by **budding**, a type of **mitosis**. A small, circular bud pushes out from the edge of the cell, like a speed bump on a road. The nucleus of the cell divides in half and one nucleus moves into the bud. The bud grows bigger and bigger until it breaks away from the original cell. Then the whole process starts again.

FROM THE FUNGUS FILES:
Coral Fungus (*Clavaria zollingeri*)

If you see small, branching antlers of purple growing under a tree, you might think you've accidentally dropped into a coral reef. Its branches are smooth and brittle, but this coral isn't from the ocean. It's a coral fungus called *Clavaria zollingeri* that grows among carpets of moss under hardwood trees in the United States and Europe. It can grow up to 4 inches (10 cm) tall and can spread up to 2 inches wide (5 cm).

Violet coral fungus can be found in the eastern forests of the United States. *Dan Molter/ Mushroom Observer*

Name That Fungus

Do you remember how Pier Antonio Micheli named an Aspergillus fungus after an aspergillum, the tool used by priests to sprinkle holy water? And how Spongiforma squarepantsii is named after the character SpongeBob SquarePants due to its sponge-like traits? People often name things in nature after other objects or living things. Now it's your turn!

MATERIALS

- 🍄 Your FUNgus Journal
- 🍄 Pencil
- 🍄 Photos from this book or a field guide

1. Take a look at these pictures of fungi. Some of them have common names, and some of them don't. What would you name them? Why?

2. Choose a fungus and draw a picture of it in your FUNgus Journal. Label it with the scientific name provided and brainstorm common names for it. Go ahead and write them in your journal. Sometimes you'll come up with several good ideas, and by combining a little of two or three ideas, you'll stumble on a great one!

3. When you're happy with one of your ideas, label the fungus with the common name.

4. Add more examples as you find them in this book or find living specimens. It's OK if you can't identify the scientific name of the fungus. You can still give it a common name.

The rare Texas star mushroom (*Choriaster geaster*) is only found in parts of Texas in the United States, and Japan. *Mason Lalley/ Mushroom Observer*

Giant puffball mushroom (*Calvatia gigantea*). *aarongunnar/Mushroom Observer*

A lattice stinkhorn mushroom with remnants of its white veil casing near the ground (*Clathrus ruber*). *Len Worthington/Mushroom Observer*

Dissect a Mushroom

The best way to learn about mushrooms is to open one up and see what's under the cap.

MATERIALS

- Your FUNgus Journal
- Pencils
- 2 or 3 white button mushrooms from a grocery store
- Paper plate or piece of paper for work surface
- Butter knife
- Magnifying glass or hand lens
- Tweezers
- Ruler

1. Draw a picture of your mushroom.

2. Write down observations about the mushroom cap: How big is it? What is its shape? What color is it? Note its texture. Is it smooth, scaly, or sticky? What does it smell like?

3. Look at the stem and write down your observations: Use a ruler to measure how wide it is. Is it hollow? What is its texture and color?

4. Turn the mushroom upside down so it is resting on its cap. If you don't see gills, then gently remove the thin layer of tissue protecting the gills. This is the veil, a thin membrane that covers the cap and stalk of an immature mushroom.

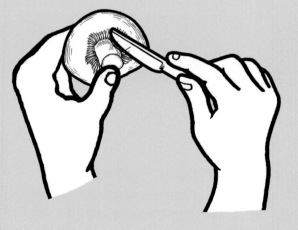

5. Now peek inside the mushroom. Use the butter knife to cut the mushroom in half from the bottom of the stalk through the cap. You should end up with two mushroom-shaped halves. Sketch what your mushroom looks like. Label the cap, gills, and stalk.

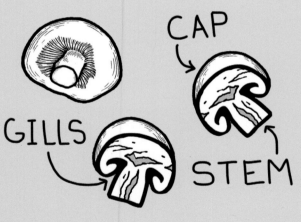

6. Get a closer look at the gills with your magnifying glass.

7. Look closer at a mushroom stalk. Select another mushroom and gently twist the stalk off. Pinch the stalk between your fingers until it breaks into two or more long pieces. Gently pull the pieces apart. The thin, hair-like filaments you will see are hyphae. Use your tweezers to pull a strip of hyphae from the stalk and look at them using your magnifying glass. Describe or draw what you see.

2

Sorting Out the Fungi

Humans have been sorting organisms into categories since the time of the ancient Greeks. Mushroom hunters and naturalists often sort fungi into groups based on shape and color. Those that produce a cap atop a stalk belong to one group, while those that resemble fans or shelves belong to another. Those collections of fungi that look alike were considered to be of the same kind, or species. Two or more species that shared traits were grouped in the same genus. Using the system developed by Carl Linnaeus, fungi

Amanita muscaria, commonly called the fly agaric, is found throughout the Northern Hemisphere.

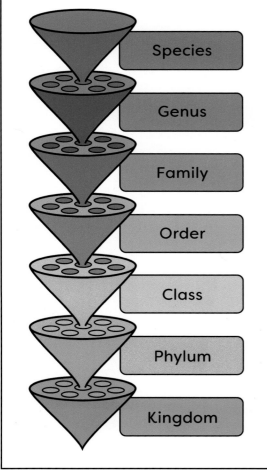

Amanita muscaria
Member of the genus *Amanita* that is large, white-spotted, and usually red.

Amanita
Amanitaceae that have pale gills, which are free from the stem and leave white spore prints.

Amanitaceae
Agaricales that have a fleshy stalk and cap.

Agaricales
Agaricomycetes that have gills.

Agaricomycetes
Basidiomycetes that produce fruiting bodies.

Basidiomycota
Fungi that produce spores on club-shaped structures.

Fungi
Organisms that have chitin in their cell walls.

sharing characteristics are grouped into families, which are grouped into orders, then classes, and finally phyla.

Seems pretty straightforward, right? There's just one small problem: mycologists are trying to sort fungi into groups without knowing how many fungi there are, and how they fit into those groups. Imagine trying to sort a box of toys while wearing a blindfold.

Each year, scientists discover more fungi. Using high-powered microscopes, they can look more closely at spores. DNA comparisons provide information about how one fungus is related to another. Over the years, scientists have sorted fungi into four, five, eight—and more—phyla. They've even gone so far as to banish certain fungus-like organisms from the kingdom.

With the help of citizen scientists, mycologists continue to discover nearly 2,000 new fungi each year—and they estimate there might still be another 2 to 3 million species waiting to be discovered. One reason they haven't found all the fungi is that so many are single-celled organisms. And fungi are secretive. They spend most of their lives hidden from sight, underground or within logs, or even inside other organisms.

Phylum Ascomycota

Around 90,000 species belong in the **phylum** Ascomycota, also called sac fungi. Mycologists informally call these fungi "ascomycetes." It's a large and diverse group, ranging from single-celled species to those with complex fruiting bodies. Blue and green molds in the genus *Penicillium* belong to this phylum, as do the yeasts that we use to make bread rise and produce alcohol. Most people notice the species that produce fruiting bodies, called ascocarps or ascomata. They may be shaped like a

MEET A MYCOLOGIST: KATHIE T. HODGE

Dr. Kathie T. Hodge is a systematic mycologist at Cornell University in Ithaca, New York. Her job focuses on the diversity and classification of fungi, particularly those associated with insects. She also manages the Cornell Plant Pathology Herbarium, a collection of 400,000 fungi specimens.

Over the past decade, Hodge has discovered and described more than 20 new species of fungi, including one that attacks millipedes. "I find things by going out and looking," she says. Like other mycologists, Hodge believes only 5 percent of fungi on Earth have been named and described.

"Mycology is a vast frontier, and there is still so much to learn," says Hodge. And while you could discover a new species in your backyard, she emphasizes that "the trick is to know whether you have truly found something new. This is where hard work and taxonomy come in."

Taxonomy is about using observational skills. What does the fungus look like? Hodge begins with a close look at the fungus.

She notes shape, size, color, and structural details. This often includes peering at her samples through a microscope. To get a closer look at spores, Hodge teases a bit of the fungus apart and puts it under high magnification. A camera attached to the microscope allows her to view enlarged images on a monitor.

"Now I can see their parts, and how they are assembled from modified hyphae," she says. "Fungi are beautiful and intricate, close up."

Hodge also analyzes the DNA of the mystery fungus. "This is like zooming in even closer," she says. "We compare sections of the DNA to genomes of known fungi in order to figure out its genetic relationships." Mycologists can also do something called "environmental sequencing" to identify DNA sequences in soil samples. That allows mycologists to gain insight into all the different fungi that live in the soil.

Want to discover a new fungus? If so, follow Hodge's tips:

- 🍄 Ask yourself: *What kind of fungi would I like to learn about?*
- 🍄 Get to know the fungi you are likely to see—build your knowledge base.
- 🍄 Look closely at fungi. "The closer you look, the more subtle differences you'll discover," she says. So take a hand lens with you when you go for a walk.

Mycologist Kathie Hodge uses a microscope to identify fungi at the annual Peck Foray. *Courtesy of Magdalen Lindeberg*

Go on a Fungal Foray

Heading off on a "fungal foray" sounds way more adventurous than going out for a mushroom walk. In most cases the only difference is the level of organization. In the past, mushroom foragers organized forays with the intention of collecting fungi for food. Many modern forays are opportunities for people to search for and learn about fungi.

As always, if you plan to go farther than your yard, ask a parent or adult to accompany you.

MATERIALS

- 🍄 Your FUNgus Journal and Explorer's Pack
- 🍄 Mushroom field guide
- 🍄 Camera
- 🍄 Water bottle (and snacks if heading out for a long time)
- 🍄 A few friends
- 🍄 If you plan to collect a few samples to study and make spore prints, you'll need paper bags for storing individual samples and a basket or box to carry your collection.

1. Choose a day for finding fungi. In the United States, mushroom season stretches from early spring through late fall, depending on temperature and rainfall.

2. Decide where you want to begin your foray. You could explore your backyard or the empty lot next door, a neighborhood park, or a nature preserve. Mushrooms can grow anywhere: in lawns, on trees, in gardens—even in flower pots. If you want to explore private property, make sure you get permission from the owner to hunt for and collect mushrooms.

3. A fungal foray can be as long—or as short—as you want it to be. Sometimes experts join forays and give brief nature talks during the walk. Others last only as long as it takes to snap photos, record observations, and collect a few samples.

4. Collect information about each of the mushrooms you find. Crack open your FUNgus Journal and make a page for each mushroom you encounter. Write the following notes:

   - The date and location (name of park, road, or address).

   - Where you find the mushroom. If it's on the ground, is it growing in grass, or did you discover it beneath leaf litter? If it's growing on wood, is it on a dead tree or a live tree? Can you identify the type of tree?

   - Is this mushroom part of a circle or a tight cluster? Or was it hanging out by itself?

   - When observing the cap, note its color, texture, and size. Is it as large as your hand or the size of your thumb? Pull out your ruler and measure the diameter.

- Does the mushroom have an odor? Some mushrooms smell like raw potatoes, while others have a fruity aroma. And some smell like rotting meat.

- Peak underneath. If there are gills, notice the color and whether they are crowded together or spaced apart. Not all mushrooms have gills. Some have pores and others have teeth.

- Take a good look at the stem. How long is it? How thick (diameter)? Note its color and texture.

- Do your fungi have bite marks or holes in them? What could be eating them? Do you see any slugs or snails, or insects or spiders living on or around the fungi?

5. When your fungal foray is finished, share what you have discovered. You can upload photos to the Mushroom Observer website (www.mushroom observer.org), a citizen scientist database, or post them on social media. If you held your foray in a local park or nature preserve, others might be interested in the data you've collected.

club or a cushion, or even like underwater corals. They can be leathery or slimy, rubbery or gelatinous, and range in color from yellow, orange, red, brown, black, and even blue.

Scarlet Caterpillar club fungi look like tiny clubs growing out of the ground. But they are actually growing from the body of an insect buried in the soil. Morels produce a conical cap, honeycombed with ridges, that sits on a broad, hollow stalk. They come in earthy colors—yellowish brown, olive, grayish black—and are highly prized by mushroom gatherers.

Cup fungi are shaped like bowls, cups, and goblets. They come in a rainbow of colors, from yellow, citrus-orange, and scarlet, to the tiny turquoise fruiting bodies of the fungi that stain wood a blue-green color. And **truffles** fruit underground, looking like alien potatoes.

As different as they look, all of the ascomycetes share a unifying feature: they produce their spores in microscopic pods or sac-like structures called asci. Most asci actively shoot their spores with great force, using the pressurized "cell sap" or cytoplasm of the ascus. In other species, the tip of each ascus has a stretchy pore.

No matter the method, the fungi in Ascomycota usually release their spores when the spores are mature and the air temperature changes to match their needs. Like most fungi, ascomycetes experience distinct daily patterns. Some release their spores at dawn, others later in the day, and some wait for a certain level of humidity in the air. Spores burst from the asci with a hiss, sometimes creating a cloud of spores above the fruiting body.

Dispersing spores by "water canon" is only one method ascomycetes use. There are huge numbers of fungi in the phylum that have lost that ability, Dr. Kathie Hodge points out, and they get their spores out

FROM THE FUNGUS FILES:
Orange Peel Fungus (*Aleuria aurantia*)

Orange peel fungus is as bright orange as its name suggests, and just like the peel of an orange, it's not something you'd want to eat. You can often find them growing in clusters on disturbed ground, such as road banks and trails, or in piles of woodchips used in landscaping. They can be found across North America.

Kingdom: Fungi
Phylum: Ascomycota
Class: Pezizomycetes
Order: Pezizales
Family: Pyronemataceae
Genus: *Aleuria*
Species: *A. aurantia*

Orange peel fungus (*Aleuria aurantia*) found around Hamburg, Germany. *Aiwok/Wikimedia Commons*

Make a Spore Print

Along with other observations, mycologists use spores to help identify unknown mushrooms. Mushroom spores can be oblong or boxy and come in a variety of colors ranging from white to olive, rusty to black. Individual spores are so tiny that you need a microscope to see them. But you can see their color and gill patterns by making a spore print.

MATERIALS

- Mushroom cap
- Paring knife
- Piece of paper (printer paper, card paper, art paper, etc.)
- Glass bowl or cup
- Hand lens
- Microscope and glass slides (optional)
- Needle (optional)
- Acrylic fixative spray or hairspray (optional)

1. Cut off the stem of the mushroom as close to where it connects with the cap as you can get.

2. Place the mushroom cap gill-side down on a smooth piece of paper. Because some mushrooms produce white spores, you might want to cover half your paper with black or dark-colored paper, so half the spores fall on the dark side.

3. Place a cup or bowl over the mushroom cap to keep air currents from disturbing it, and leave it overnight. The spores will fall on the paper.

4. The following day, gently lift the mushroom cap off the paper and you'll see a pattern.

5. Compare spore prints from different kinds of mushrooms. What do you notice about the pattern and color of spores? Look at the spores through a hand lens. Can you see individual spores?

6. (Optional) If you have a microscope, make a slide to look at individual spores. Use a needle to scrape some spores from your spore print onto a glass slide. Put a drop of water on the spores and cover with a cover slip.

7. (Optional) To preserve your spore print, spray it with acrylic fixative or hairspray. Make sure to hold the spray at least a foot away from the paper so you don't blow the spores away.

8. (Optional) You can also make spore prints using mushrooms that release their spores from pores. Soft mushrooms on stems may produce better spore prints than harder polypore mushrooms. Put on your lab coat, pull out your FUNgus Journal, and do some spore print experiments. Try making art by overlapping spore prints. Discover what happens when you don't cover the cap while spores are dropping.

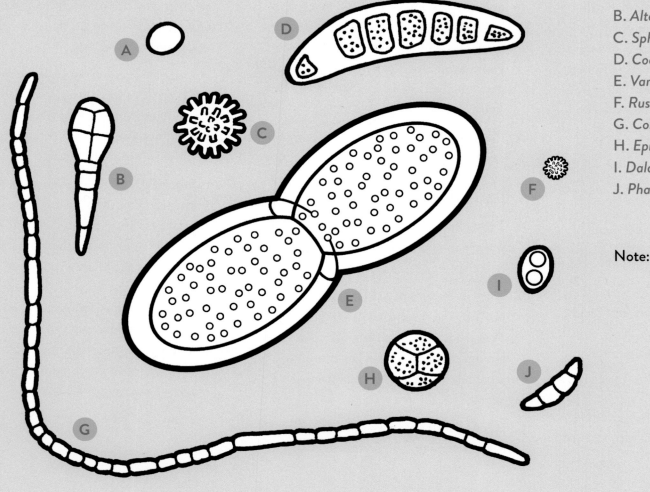

Here are just a few depictions of the great variety of fungus spores!

A. *Ganoderma applanatum*
B. *Alternaria alternata*
C. *Sphaerosoma echinulatum*
D. *Cochliobolus sativus*
E. *Varicellaria rhodocarpa*
F. *Russula diffusa*
G. *Cordyceps pseudolloydii*
H. *Epicoccum nigrum*
I. *Daldinia Concentrica*
J. *Phaesosphaeria nodorum*

Note: spores not drawn to scale.

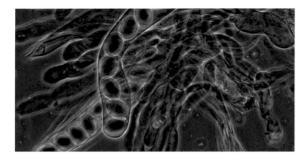

Asci and spores of a morel mushroom (*Morchella elata*). *Peter G. Werner/Wikimedia Commons*

another way. Truffles are one example. Truffles grow completely underground and depend on animals for spore dispersal. Once truffle spores are mature, the truffles release odors that attract squirrels, deer, and other animals. The animals eat the fungus, spores and all, then deposit the

spores in their droppings. Truffle spores have thick walls of chitin that protect them during their journey through animal digestive tracts.

Phylum Basidiomycota

The second-largest group of fungi, boasting nearly 50,000 known species, is the phylum Basidiomycota. They are also called "club fungi" because they produce their spores on club-shaped cells called basidia. Each basidia contains four spores but, in contrast to ascomycetes, these spores are produced on the outside of the structure. Instead of shooting out of pods, these spores fall when they are released, relying on air currents to carry them. If they're lucky, they'll land in a place where they can grow.

Bolete mushrooms have pores under their caps instead of gills. *Ron Pastorino/Mushroom Observer*

Basidiomycota are found in nearly all ecosystems, including freshwater and saltwater habitats, in addition to soils. They range from single-celled yeasts to large and complex fruiting bodies. Most of the large fungi we call "mushrooms" are basidiomycetes. They have domed or flattened caps attached to a stalk. Gilled mushrooms, called agarics, have paper-thin **gills** beneath the caps, radiating from the stalk to the edge of the cap. When the spores are mature, they fall through the spaces between the gills, with up to several hundred spores released per minute. This group contains the edible button mushrooms you can buy in a grocery store (*Agaricus bisporus*) as well as some of the most poisonous mushrooms, including the death cap (*Amanita phalloides*).

Bolete mushrooms also have a cap and stalk, but when you look underneath, they have no gills. Instead, the underside is filled with pores. Each pore is an opening of a long, vertical tube in which the spores are made. Bracket fungi and shelf fungi also form large fruiting bodies with pores on the underside. Unlike boletes, they have no stems and grow directly out of tree trunks and decaying logs. Some, known as Chicken of the Woods, are yellow and orange like candy corn, while others look more like the turkey tails they are named after.

There are mushrooms that look like trumpets and some that have toothlike spines instead of gills under their caps. Some resemble underwater coral and others look like gelatinous globs of jelly.

Not all basidiomycetes release spores into the air. Puffballs and earthstars grow their spore-producing basidia inside a round fruiting body. They need something to trigger the spore dispersal. Sometimes, all it takes is a small animal brushing against it, or the plop of raindrops, to distribute a dust cloud of spores into the air.

Bird's nest fungi are about the size of your pinky nail and look like miniature bird's nests when mature. The basidia and spores grow inside egg-shaped packets. When a raindrop falls—splash!—a spore-filled egg flies out of the nest and lands nearby.

Stinkhorns are aptly named: they smell! These fungi produce their spores in a stinky mass of slime that smells like a carcass, feces, or flowers to attract flies and other insects. When an insect climbs in for a snack, spores stick to its feet and other body parts.

FROM THE FUNGUS FILES:
Bioluminescent Fungi

Scientists have identified more than 75 species of bioluminescent (glow-in-the-dark) fungi. All the known species are saprobes, a type of fungi that can decompose wood. Bioluminescent fungi contain the same chemicals that cause fireflies to glow, though no one has discovered why mushrooms glow in the dark. In some environments the glow could discourage animals and insects from grazing on the mushroom, while in others, it might attract the right animals to help spread mature spores. Although this particular species, *Mycena chlorophos,* is found in subtropical Asia, Australia, and Brazil, you can find many members of the family in North America and Europe. Just look for a pale green light glowing in the woods at night.

Kingdom: Fungi
Phylum: Basidiomycota
Class: Agaricomycetes
Order: Agaricales
Family: Mycenaceae
Genus: *Mycena*
Species: *M. chlorophos*

Glow-in-the-dark mushrooms (*Mycena chlorophos*) in New South Wales, Australia.
Steve Axford/Mushroom Observer

Build a Simple Microscope

If you want to see mushrooms—and spores—up close, you need a microscope. Magnification allows you to notice tiny details that you can't see with your bare eye. If you don't have a microscope, you can make one using common household items.

MATERIALS

- White index card or other small piece of paper
- Two pencils
- Long piece of clear or transparent tape
- Eyedropper or straw
- Water
- FUNgus Journal

1. Place the small piece of white paper on a counter.

2. Put the pencils on either side of the paper.

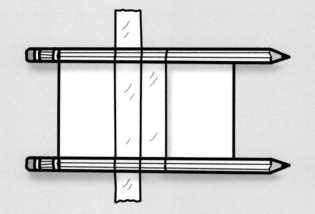

3. Stretch a long piece of tape over the pencils, making sure to tape them to the counter. The tape should stay tight.

4. Slide a small piece of a mushroom, lichen, or even a plant below the tape. Be sure it's small enough that it won't stick to the tape!

5. Using the eyedropper or straw, place one drop of water on the tape above the object. Take a look. Are you able to see more details?

6. Try adding a drop at a time until you have about four or five drops on the tape. As you add each drop, look at the object. Does it get clearer? Do you notice more details?

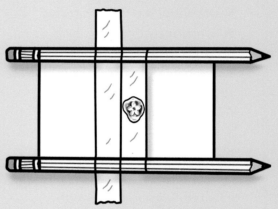

7. Make a note in your journal reminding you how many drops of water you needed to see the object most clearly. Anytime you want to take a close look at something, assemble your simple microscope and jot down the things you notice when it's magnified under your microscope.

FROM THE FUNGUS FILES:
Amphibian Chytrid Fungus

The fungus *Batrachochytrium dendrobatidis* infects the part of a frog's skin that contain keratin. Frogs use their skin to breathe, and the fungus creates skin lesions that makes it hard for frogs to breathe. The fungus also infects the nervous system, affecting the frog's behavior. Sick frogs are often lethargic, sitting in the open instead of hiding from predators. And researchers have found that in some species, infected frogs produce longer calls.

Kingdom: Fungi
Phylum: Chytridiomycota
Class: Chytridiomycetes
Order: Rhizophydiales
Genus: *Batrachochytrium*
Species: *B. dendrobatidis*

As it flies away, the insect carries spores to a new home. And some spores can survive insect digestion to be deposited alive, in insect poop.

Phylum Chytridiomycota

Scientists have found almost a thousand species of fungi that belong to this phylum—so far. They are microscopic and generally live in aquatic or moist habitats. Chytrid fungi have been discovered in bogs and ponds, rivers and ditches, and in forest soils, from the tropics all the way to the North Pole. Scientists describe them as single-celled organisms even though they may produce rootlike structures that anchor

them to a food source. They produce spores that have a single taillike **flagellum.** That tail comes in handy when the spores need to swim to a better location.

Some chytrids feast on plant and animal debris, digesting stuff that other fungi cannot break down, such as keratin and chitin. Others are **pathogens** of algae and crops, such as corn and potatoes, as well as animals. One species, *Batrachochytrium dendrobatidis*, infects amphibians and is responsible for mass die-offs of frogs.

Phylum Mucoromycota

Most of the species of fungi in Mucoromycota are microscopic. They are usually

Frog infected with chytrid fungus.
Brian Gratwicke/ Wikimedia Commons

Design Your Own Fungus

As you've seen, fungi come in a variety of shapes, colors, and sizes. Some resemble living things such as coral or cauliflower. Others look like body parts, like ears, eyes, and fingers! Some mushrooms might have inspired inventors to create umbrellas, cups, bowls, or soccer balls.

   Now it's your chance to dream up a unique fungus.

MATERIALS

- 🍄 Your FUNgus Journal
- 🍄 Pencil
- 🍄 Colored pencils, markers, or paint

1. Create a fungus and draw it in your journal. It can be beautiful or strange, camouflaged or bright.

2. Make up a name for your new fungus. Consider what it looks like, how it smells, and its texture. For example, you might name a red mushroom after your friend: *Rubeus jimbobii*

Here are some Latin root words to get you inspired:

red: *rubeus* or *scarlatinus*	**hard:** *dura*
yellow: *flavus* or *citrinus*	**soft:** *mollis*
green: *viridis* or *chlorum*	**round:** *circum*
blue: *caeruleus*	**flat:** *planus*
pink: *roseus*	**beautiful:** *formosus*
large: *magnis*	**waxy:** *cera*
small: *parvus*	**sticky:** *viscosa*

associated with plants and include species that live inside plants. The group includes some of the molds that grow on breads and fruits as well as fungi that form symbiotic relationships with the roots of plants. If you looked at a scoop of soil beneath a microscope, you would see many species of Mucoromycota.

Phylum Microsporidia

There are about 1,300 named species of fungi placed in the phylum Microsporidia. They are one-celled **parasites** that infect the guts, skin, and muscles of insects, fish, and many other animals. One species, *Nosema ceranae,* parasitizes honeybees, shortening their lives. Microsporidians also infect people, causing diarrhea, kidney disease, and sinus and eye infections. At one time they were considered to be protozoans, like amoebas. But a genetic analysis showed that they contain the genes to make chitin, a characteristic of all fungi. Scientists also found chitin in their spores.

Not Fungi

Water molds (oomycetes) and slime molds look a lot like fungi, but they are two very different organisms.

FROM THE FUNGUS FILES:
The Hat Thrower Fungus (*Pilobolus crystallinus*)

The Hat Thrower knows how to put the FUN in fungus. These tiny fungi develop on fresh deposits of cow, sheep, and horse dung. If you looked at a splat of cow dung after three or four days, you'd notice a miniature forest of spore-bearing stalks.

When the spores are mature, the fungus flings them upward about 6 feet (2 m) high at speeds up to 56 miles per hour (25 meters per second). That's like a person throwing a football more than 300 yards (275 m).

What's even cooler: these fungi can determine the direction to fling their spores based on the sun's position. Sunlight means fresh vegetation. Spores landing on that vegetation are more likely to be eaten by grazing animals and deposited far away from their original dung home. This ensures that the fungus aims its spores at the animals' likely next meal.

Kingdom: Fungi
Phylum: Mucoromycota (Zygomycota)
Class: Mucoromycotina
Order: Mucorales
Family: Pilobolaceae
Genus: *Pilobolus*
Species: *P. crystallinus*

Hat Thrower fungi growing on sheep dung.
Sava Krstic/Mushroom Observer

Oomycetes have branched, threadlike filaments that resemble fungal hyphae, and they live in the same habitats as fungi. They even produce spores. But they do not have chitin in their cell walls. Instead, their cell walls are made of cellulose-like **compounds**. And when you look at them under the microscope, you see that oomycete filaments don't have any cross-walls or partitions like fungal hyphae. They are related to certain algae, but they've traded the ability to photosynthesize for the lifestyle of a pathogen.

Slime molds, too, produce clusters of spores, and at one time they were even classified as fungi. They may look moldy, but they don't have chitin in their cell walls. Slime molds, it turns out, are more closely related to amoebas.

3

Fungi Hold the World Together

Thousands of bits of fungal hyphae and mycelial threads can be found in a gram of soil, or about a teaspoonful. Separated and laid end to end, those threads might stretch a few hundred feet—or a few miles. Up to 100,000 microscopic spores could be on your spoon, any of which could start growing a new colony.

Lichens and other fungi together on a branch. *Courtesy of Steve Hall*

Mushrooms in the wild. *Courtesy of Terrie Crance*

Tangled, the mycelium helps bind soil particles into crumb-sized clumps. Those clumps, called aggregates, play a vital role in soil health. They increase the amount of water soil can absorb and help reduce the amount of nutrients leached out of the soil.

Landscape Architects

Some scientists consider fungi "ecosystem engineers" because of the way they help shape the landscape. After forest fires,

some species of morels and cup fungi are among the first living things to appear amid the ash. Within a few weeks these fungi mature and produce fruiting bodies that release spores. They also release fragrances that attract insects and other animals. Flies arrive to deposit their eggs in the mushrooms. Birds are attracted to the hatched larvae. Other mushroom-eating animals drop by to snack as well, leaving splats and piles of see-bearing poop from other places.

Fossils provide evidence that fungi have been poking their hyphae into the landscaping business for millions of years. Plants and fungi migrated together, as partners, from sea onto land around 500 million years ago. Those early plants had no roots. Instead, fungi grew inside the plants, stabilizing them by plunging their hyphae into the rocky substrate. Fungi dissolved the rocks, absorbing minerals that plants needed to grow. In return, the plants provided the fungi with food produced through photosynthesis.

As with other stories laid down in the fossil record, the story of fungi was not rock solid. In 2014, Robert Rainbird discovered even older fungal fossils dating back nearly a billion years. Rainbird, a research scientist with the Geological Survey of Canada, specializes in sediments. While collecting shale samples in the Canadian Arctic, he noticed black flecks in them and wondered whether those flecks were microscopic fossils.

Although Rainbird could determine the age of the rock, he could not tell exactly what the smudges were. He sent samples to other scientists to identify them. One of those scientists was Corentin Loron.

Loron dunked the rocks into an acid bath to separate the smudges from the rock. He ended up with a black paste, which he smeared on a glass slide. When he put it

under a microscope, Loron saw hundreds of microfossils. They were single-celled, but much bigger than bacteria. Additional samples showed that the spherical structures had double walls. When scientists examined the microfossils using infrared light, they determined that the spheres were made of chitin, a distinguishing feature of fungi.

If fungi were colonizing the land before plants evolved, they had plenty of time to engineer a plant-friendly environment. But without plants, what did the ancient fungi eat?

Nature's Recyclers

Researchers think the ancient fungi probably ate bacterial crusts that grew over the earth's surface. As **heterotrophs**, fungi get their energy from other living organisms. They eat, or digest, plants and animals as well as the things left behind, such as dead skin cells, dung, pollen, and leaves. Without fungi, branches, logs, and dead plants would pile up. So would the carcasses of dead animals. Yuck!

Imagine a world without fungi. A single deciduous tree produces around a million leaves every year. If you could put them on a scale, they would weigh about

440 pounds (200 kg). Let them pile up year after year, and after five years you'd have a knee-deep layer of leaves covering the ground. Not only would it be hard to walk around, but such a thick layer of dead leaves would keep new plants from growing. Smart gardeners know this and pile leaves on their vegetable beds to prevent weeds from sprouting.

Decomposer fungi are also called **saprotrophs**. They, along with a few bacteria, are the only organisms able to break down the cellulose and lignin in dead wood and plants. Lignin is the component that makes wood rigid, and it is hard to digest.

Around 300 million years ago, a group of fungi evolved the ability to break down that lignin. Known as "white rot fungi," they produce strong enzymes—proteins that help speed up chemical reactions. The enzymes break apart the chemical bonds in lignin, releasing carbon dioxide and leaving behind simple sugars. With the lignin bonds broken, other organisms can break apart the remaining plant material.

Breaking down complex molecules makes nutrients available to other organisms. This is how nutrients and minerals are recycled and incorporated back into the food chain.

What Happens If You Don't Rake the Grass?

Left on their own, short grass clippings decompose. They add nutrients to the soil and help it retain water. The best way to find out how fast your grass decomposes is to leave some on your lawn. Just make sure the grass isn't treated with chemicals.

MATERIALS

- Wooden skewers or old chopsticks
- Permanent marker
- Masking tape
- Your FUNgus Journal
- Thermometer (if you have one)
- Ruler
- Places where you can leave piles of grass

1. Get permission to leave a section of grass unraked. If you don't have a lawn, you can pile clippings along the edge of a driveway or sidewalk.

2. The next time your lawn gets mowed, mark a spot with a skewer or chopstick. Write the date and a letter (A, B, C . . .) on masking tape and tape it to the stick. Then write down in your notebook the date and the letter "name" of that grass pile plus any notes. If you have a thermometer, put it in the clippings and jot down the temperature.

3. Rake up some clippings and create a grass pile that is about an inch deep. Write the date and a different letter on masking tape and mark the spot with a labeled stick. Make sure to write down a description including how high the pile is. If you have a thermometer, put it in the clippings and jot down the temperature.

4. Check your clippings a couple times a week. Jot down notes about the weather: Has it rained? Was it hot? Measure the height of the piles and the temperature inside of them. What is happening to the grass on the surface of the pile? What's happening to the lawn under the piles? After a few days you might see thin strands of fungi and slimy grass.

5. When it's time to mow the lawn again, examine the area where the original layer of clippings was left. Have they decomposed?

6. (Optional) Other things to explore: What happens if you make a pile that is half cut grass and half dead leaves? What happens if you let the grass dry a day before raking it into higher piles?

Fungi for Dinner

Fungi play another important role in the food web—they provide food for a wide range of organisms. Animals eat the fruity parts of fungi: the mushrooms, puffballs, morels, and truffles. If you're walking through a wooded area and notice spots where leaves have been disturbed, take a closer look. Perhaps squirrels have been digging for mushrooms. Red squirrels have been known to collect and dry mushrooms and store them in nooks and crevices of tree branches.

Around the world, a diversity of animals munch on mushrooms for their meals: gorillas, lemurs, marmosets, elk, and even turtles and shrews. Moose and reindeer graze on fungi, as do kangaroos, wallabies, and wombats. Chipmunks, deer, skunks, and armadillos feast on fungi as well, and birds and boars have been known to dig for truffles.

Snails and slugs scrape their way across mushrooms, and one species of ant chews off pieces of mushroom to carry back to the nest. Other insects eat the fruiting bodies and spores, but fungus gnat larvae nosh on thin fungal filaments in the soil. And while most millipedes eat decomposing plant matter, some dine exclusively on fungi.

Some insects have an agricultural relationship with their fungal food. African termite societies have been cultivating mushrooms in underground chambers for the past 30 million years. Foraging termites collect spores of the fungus *Termitomyces*, along with the grass, leaves, and wood they chow down on. Back at the mound, the plant material is pooped out to create a spot to plant the fungus. Then the termites mix in the spores and tend their gardens. Fungal enzymes break down woody plant fibers, spreading mycelium throughout the garden. After a few weeks, the termites

FROM THE FUNGUS FILES:
Turkey Tail (*Trametes versicolor*)

It's easy to see how these mushrooms get their name. Turkey tail mushrooms are flat and wavy fan-shaped fungi that look just like the striped feathers in the tails of turkeys. They are paper-thin shelf fungi, only ⅒th of an inch (1–3 mm) thick. Turkey tails are also important recyclers of dead wood. Next time you pick up a piece of rotted wood, notice how light it is. That's because fungi have digested all the heavy lignin.

Around the 1950s, paper industry researchers began testing whether turkey tail fungi might provide a nonchemical alternative in the wood-pulping process. Turkey tail fungi leave cellulose intact, and cellulose is the part of wood that is used to make paper. This fungus can also degrade some of the pesticides that tend to stick around in the environment.

Turkey tail mushrooms grow on dead deciduous logs and trees.
Megan Ralph/Mushroom Observer

A leafcutter ant carries a leaf, and a hitch-hiker, back to the nest. *Sam May/Flickr*

consume tiny pin mushrooms, mycelium, and used up compost. Once a year, the fungus gardens produce mushrooms that push out of the termite mound, so there's always a ready supply of spores.

Halfway around the world, in the Americas and Caribbean, leafcutter ants do the farming. They snip pieces of leaves with their sharp mandibles, carrying them home like huge green umbrellas. Once they return to their underground nests, the ants chew up the leaves and add them to their fungus garden. They tend to the fungus and feed it to their larvae.

Ants are careful gardeners. They fertilize their crop when needed and pull out "weeds"—unwanted fungi that compete with their main crop. They also keep mites and other fungus-nibbling pests from snacking on the garden. While the cultivated fungus thrives in the ant nest, it can't survive outside of this environment. So, when a young queen heads off to start a new colony, she takes part of the fungus with her to start her own garden.

Ambrosia beetles, members of the weevil family, cultivate their fungus gardens inside trees. They gnaw galleries in dead or dying trees and use the tunnel walls as a hanging garden. The fungus is the sole source of food for the beetles and their larvae.

Plant Partners

More than 90 percent of the Earth's plant species depend on fungi. Fungi live in the root zone of trees and other plants and form a **symbiotic** relationship. Due to their close relationship, people refer to it as **mycorrhizal**—a combination of "myco" for fungi and "rhizome" for root zone.

Fungi expand the reach of the plant's root system. They help carry water and nutrients, such as nitrogen and phosphorus, to plant roots. Fungal mycelium spans outward like a cobweb, creating a dense mat of interconnected threads. That mycelial web increases a root's surface area, allowing it to absorb more nutrients from the soil than a root without mycorrhizae. In exchange, the trees and plants provide energy in the form of carbohydrates to the fungi.

In some cases, the interconnected mycelium forms a network between several plants. This allows the plants to share limited supplies of water and nutrients with one another. Sometimes, for example, older trees give younger seedlings a boost. Trees even send nutrients to different species. In one study, scientists found that Douglas fir seedlings and paper birch shared carbohydrates through the mycorrhizal network. During the summer, when the Douglas fir seedlings were shaded by the forest canopy, paper birch sent nutrients. In spring and fall, when the birch trees had no leaves, the Douglas fir sent carbohydrates to them.

Trees aren't the only ones to send food and messages through a mycelial network. Grassland plants do too. Some wildflowers form a relationship with fungi. These flowers have no chlorophyll, so they can't make their own food. They depend on fungi for all their nutritional needs. Or, rather, they depend on fungi to act as a food transfer station. The fungi provide minerals and nutrients to the trees in exchange for carbohydrates, which they pass on to the flowers.

In exchange, the flowers give the fungi . . . nothing. It's a one-sided food friendship that allows the flowers to thrive in the deepest, shadiest part of the forest.

Because they depend on fungi for food, these flowers are called **mycotrophic**. They spend most of their lives underground, poking through the soil and leaf litter only when it's time to flower. With no chlorophyll, their stems and flowers display a rainbow of colors from ghostly white, to yellows and oranges, and even deep red. What leaves they produce tend to be small and scalelike, giving their stems the appearance of alien asparagus. Despite their unusual appearance, these wildflowers bloom, produce pollen, and eventually go to seed.

THE WOOD WIDE WEB

Trees use the underground fungal network to share food and water. They also send chemical and electrical signals through the mycelium to warn other trees of insect attacks or disease. So perhaps it was only a matter of time before someone began referring to the underground forest network as the "wood wide web." Dr. Suzanne Simard, a forest ecologist from the University of British Columbia, came up with the name to describe the relationships she discovered between the Douglas firs and other trees she studied.

These trees are connected in a mycorrhizal network.

Fold a Fungus Bookmark

After you make this cute mushroom book-mark, place it over the corner of a page and you'll never lose your place again! Use origami paper, giftwrap, or other interesting paper to fold a colorful mushroom!

MATERIALS

- 6 inch x 6 inch paper (or other size square paper)
- Pencil
- Scissors
- Colored pencils, crayons, or markers

1. Put your square of paper on the table, design-side down. Turn the square so it looks like a diamond. Fold the bottom corner up to the top and press the fold to make a triangle.

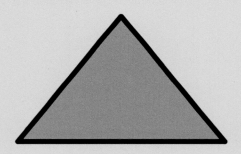

2. Bring the right corner up to the top point of the triangle and fold. Do the same with the left corner. Now it should look like a diamond.

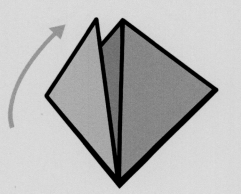

3. Open the most recent folds to see the large triangle again, then bring one flap down from the top point to meet the bottom edge.

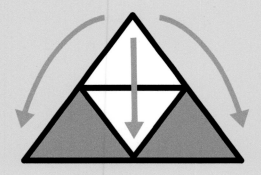

4. Fold the bottom right point of the tri-angle up to the top point. Repeat with the bottom left point, so that the two points meet at the top of the diamond.

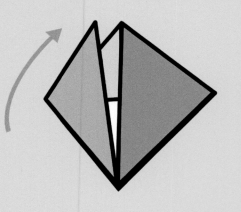

5. Fold the right point back and tuck it behind the folded-down flap to make a pocket. Do the same with the left corner.

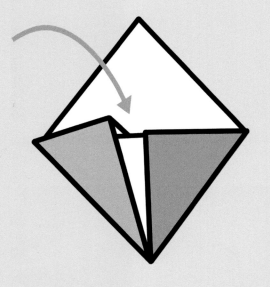

6. Turn the paper around so the white corner is at the bottom and the folded section is the top. The folded part is your mushroom cap. Draw a stem on the unfolded part.

7. Cut out the area around the stem and decorate your mushroom.

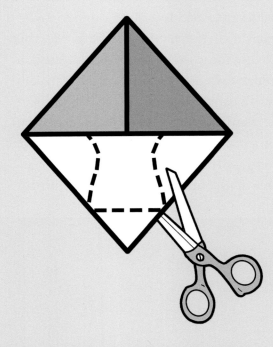

8. Slide your bookmark over the corner of the page before you close the book to hold your place!

Lichen Associations

A lichen may look like a single organism, but it's a cooperative living arrangement between fungi and green algae or cyanobacteria. Green algae and cyanobacteria produce their own food through photosynthesis, providing food for their fungal partners. In return, fungi create a structure to protect their photosynthetic partners from sunburn and drying out.

Heinrich Anton de Bary, a German surgeon, botanist, and early mycologist, was fascinated by lichens. In 1879 he coined a term to describe the living together of unlike organisms. He called it symbiosis. He used the term to denote a close, long-term relationship between two organisms. Most people use the word to refer to **mutualism**, in which each organism benefits. But in some relationships, only one partner benefits.

Until 2016, a lichen was understood to be a partnership between one alga and one fungus. Then, scientists announced that they had found a yeast that was a third

Pink Indian Pipes blooming in a New Hampshire forest. *Magellan/Wikimedia Commons*

MEET THE MYCOTROPHS

Ghost plants (*Monotropa uniflora*) look like clusters of pale, waxy stems sprouting from a layer of leaf litter. The stems reach from 4 to 12 inches tall (10–30 cm), bearing thin, translucent leaves and a single bell-shaped flower drooping from the end. A favorite flower of poet Emily Dickinson, ghost plants grow across most of the United States and Canada. Scientists set up remote video cameras to find out how fungus flowers were pollinated. They discovered that bumblebees are the major visitors. Once pollinated, the stem straightens and each flower forms a pod. When it opens, the tiny seeds are carried on the wind.

Bristly beard lichen found on a pear tree. *Sue Heavenrich/Author photo*

Leafy lichens growing on a stone wall in Vermont. *Sue Heavenrich/Author photo*

Lichen-Looking Expedition

Lichen can be found most anywhere: on trees and rocks, a sidewalk, or a wooden planter— even on gravestones in a nearby cemetery. So go explore!

MATERIALS

- Your Explorer's Pack and FUNgus Journal
- Lichen field guide or smart phone (mushroomobserver.org)
- Spray bottle with water
- Camera

1. Grab your Explorer's Pack and your FUNgus Journal as well as a lichen field guide (you could also go to www .mushroomobserver.org if you have a smartphone and phone service), then choose an outdoor spot to conduct your search.

2. When you find something that looks like a lichen, spritz it with some water. Moisture helps the lichen's true colors show. Then take a photo or draw a picture.

3. Make a page in your journal to write about this lichen. Write down the date and where you are.

4. Describe what your lichen looks like. Is it leafy? Crusty? Branchy? What color is it? Measure it with your ruler.

5. Where's this lichen growing? How high above the ground? If it is on a tree, can you determine what side of the tree it's growing on: north, south, east, or west?

6. Is your lichen growing by itself or are there other lichens growing next to it? Are those lichens the same type? Are there nonlichen things growing in the same place, such as moss?

7. Are there insects, spiders, or other tiny animals living in and around your lichen? Look closely; you might discover some mushrooms growing with them.

FROM THE FUNGUS FILES:
Using Lichens in the Chemistry Lab

Have you ever used litmus paper to test whether something is an **acid** or a **base**? If so, you've used a lichen dye. One of the lichens commonly used is the crustose *Ochrolechia tartarea*. Once harvested and dried, the lichens are pulverized, treated with chemicals, and left to ferment.

Litmus paper is blue because it has been soaked with the lichen solution and dried. When dipped into an acid, such as lemon juice, the paper turns red. Another type of litmus paper is mixed with an acid when it is made. This red litmus paper turns blue when dipped into a solution of baking soda and water.

This is one of the crustose lichens used to dye litmus paper. *Zaca Lepista/Mushroom Observer*

USING LICHENS AS CAMOUFLAGE

Green lacewing larvae love to eat aphids. But with ants guarding the sweet food source, how's a hungry bug to get a meal? By donning a disguise! The lacewing larvae secretes sticky silk on its back, trapping tiny pieces of lichen. Suitably camouflaged, the lacewing can sneak right by the ants and feast on aphids. As for the lichens, any pieces that fall off might find an inviting spot to start growing.

This green lacewing larva attaches lichen to its back for camouflage. *Judy Gallagher/Flickr*

symbiotic partner in many lichens. Ecologist Merlin Sheldrake suggests that lichens are microbiomes. Just as a forest **biome** is filled with a community of plants and animals, lichens are home to fungi and bacteria in addition to the symbiotic partners. A biome on a very tiny scale!

Lichens come in a variety of growth forms. Fruticose lichens look like lacy tumbleweeds or tiny, branched shrubs. Some look like tiny cups on stalks, others hang like filaments from branches. And some, like British soldier lichen, stand upright with what look like red hats on their heads.

Crustose lichens form thick, rough crusts on rocks, bark, monuments, even roof shingles. Some boast bright colors, looking more like splats of bright yellow, orange, and red paint than a living organism. Others are gray and green, blending into the environment.

Foliose lichens look like leafy lobes in subdued hues of green and gray. You might find them growing among moss or surrounding the branch of a bush. Some lichens incorporate a mix of growth forms. Squamulose lichens, which look like tiny shingles attached to the surface, combine features of foliose and crustose growth forms. Filamentous lichens look like matted hair, while other lichens look like nothing more than powder sprinkled over a section of bark.

Lichens are "ecosystem pioneers." They are the first to colonize volcanoes and bare rock. The fungal hyphae grow into the rock, digesting the minerals and contributing to the weathering process. Lichens trap dust and silt that blow across rocky surfaces, and mosses take root in the accumulating material. As lichens die and decay, they contribute to the first soils in a new ecosystem.

Because of their ability to exist in extreme environments, lichens are found everywhere on Earth. They live on the tundra, in Antarctica, and even at the tide line of ocean cliffs. Crustose lichens living on hot desert floors help stabilize the soil, reducing sandstorms.

4

Fungi as Food

We're always told to eat our fruits and vegetables, but when was the last time you were reminded to eat your mushrooms? Mushrooms taste good and they're good for you! They're full of protein and vitamin D as well as amino acids, potassium, magnesium, calcium, zinc, and more.

Mushrooms are also low in fat, cholesterol, and sodium. Not only that, they're gluten free. Many foods and drinks rely on fungi for **fermentation**, so you may be consuming fungi without even knowing it!

Button mushrooms (*Agaricus bisporus*) are delicious and plentiful.
Bob Peters/Wikimedia Commons

Button Mushrooms

Imagine discovering small, brown mushrooms pushing their rounded tops from a pile of manure. Would that make you think of lunch? Yuck! But according to historical accounts, more than 300 years ago in France, that's exactly how people discovered one of the most popular mushrooms eaten today. That mushroom is *Agaricus bisporus*, a brownish button mushroom. When harvested young, it's called a cremini mushroom, but when fully mature, is known as a portobello mushroom. Later, in the 1920s, a mushroom farmer in Pennsylvania found a white version of the button mushroom and cultivated it because it looked nice.

The mushrooms for sale in the grocery store or sliced on a pizza are probably button mushrooms. Button mushrooms account for over 90 percent of the mushrooms eaten in the United States. Specialty mushrooms are becoming more popular, though. Some growers offer specialty mushrooms such as shiitake, lion's mane, cordyceps, maitake, oyster, and enoki. Each kind of mushroom requires special growing conditions, though, which is why some people shy away from committing their time and resources to cultivating them. Shiitake mushrooms can be grown outdoors on logs in the wooded northeastern and northwestern United States, though some growers prefer to use beds of sawdust. Other species, including oyster mushrooms, lion's mane, and other specialty mushrooms require certain temperatures and humidity to fruit, conditions that outdoor culture may not meet. This is one reason many mushroom farmers choose to cultivate their crop indoors. While they can control the temperature and humidity indoors, growers must also make sure they provide the right type of light and air flow for each species.

Growing mushrooms is a bit different than growing vegetables in a garden. A big concern is keeping pests, including other microorganisms, out of the mushroom beds. Growers do this by sterilizing the substrate, a growing medium such as sawdust, straw, or waste paper. Then they add the mushroom spawn. Once the mycelium from the spawn covers the substrate, mushroom fruiting can begin.

Spawn is a blend of fungal spores and a nutrient source, often a grain. Adding spawn to compost is like adding sourdough starter to bread dough—it kick-starts the growing.

When it's time to harvest the mushrooms, the growers use a knife or scissors to slice the stems as close to the substrate as possible. More mushrooms will usually grow on the substrate over the following weeks.

It sounds complicated, but some growers don't do everything themselves. There are companies that specialize in preparing spawn for commercial use or home kits. Some growers buy blocks of medium or they buy logs that have already had the mycelium of the mushroom variety they want to grow added. That allows growers to focus on tending the crop and harvesting mushrooms.

Commercial Mushroom Farming

Maryland's Warwick Mushroom Farms is the largest mushroom growing facility in the Western Hemisphere. From the outside, the farm's three large steel buildings look like industrial warehouses. Inside, the space is divided into growing rooms, each furnished with wide, aluminum shelves stacked six high from floor to ceiling. Altogether, they provide more growing area than 14 football fields. Wide aisles separate the stacks, and a computerized

system controls the temperature, humidity, and levels of carbon dioxide for each room.

Making a mushroom bed takes more than a rake and a hoe. Compost inoculated with mushroom spawn is moved by conveyor onto the steel shelves.

The fungi begin growing, spreading mycelium throughout the compost. After twelve days, the growers force the fungi to fruit by lowering the level of carbon dioxide to a fraction of what it was. The first tiny mushrooms are no bigger than pinheads, but they double in size every 24 hours. In less than a week, the first crop is ready to pick.

Each mushroom harvester has a motorized vehicle with a lift that raises them up to the high beds. Mushrooms bruise easily, so harvesters pick, weigh, and pack them as they go. And because the fruiting bodies grow so quickly, each room is harvested multiple times a day. Two weeks later, a second flush of mushrooms is produced and, after another two weeks, the third and final growth.

Once the last mushroom is harvested, the compost is removed and shipped to local farms where it's spread on fields to improve the soil. The shelves and room are sterilized and growers get ready for the next crop.

In the course of a year, a single growing room cycles through six and a half crops. With 72 growing rooms, that adds up; in 2020, Warwick Mushroom Farms produced 32 million pounds of mushrooms. To keep up with that rate of production they employ 300 people, including growers, harvesters, engineers, and computer techs.

Farming Mushrooms in the Forest

The first thing you notice at Hawk Meadow Farm, in Trumansburg, New York, is the yellow farmhouse with chickens pecking in the yard. In 2006, a powerful windstorm knocked down hundreds of trees in the surrounding woods. After cutting firewood and milling lumber, Steve Sierigk wondered whether he could use some of the downed trees to grow mushrooms. He'd successfully raised shiitake mushrooms on a small scale, but could he translate that experience into a commercial venture?

What's for Sale?

Now that you're learning more about edible mushrooms, you may want to try cooking and eating some. Grab your FUNgus journal and take stock of what's available at your favorite store or farmer's market.

MATERIALS

- 🍄 Ruler
- 🍄 Pencil
- 🍄 Your FUNgus Journal

1. Visit the produce section of a grocery store or farmer's market. Locate the mushrooms. How many different types of mushrooms are for sale?

2. Using a ruler, draw in your journal a horizontal row for each kind of mushroom sold (regular, organic, small button, large portobello, oyster, etc.).

3. Now create vertical columns and record how many packages of each are on the shelves, how many ounces in each container, and the price for each.

4. Write down your observations. Which ones appear to sell fastest? Is there shelf space for more? Do the mushrooms look firm and fresh? How many different varieties are available? Why do you think that is?

That winter Steve and his wife, Anne, sawed trees into logs. "Shiitake mushrooms are sapwood feeders," Steve explains. They'll grow on oak, beech, chestnut, and other wood.

Steve and Anne drilled holes into logs and poured a mix of sawdust and shiitake mushroom mycelium into each hole. They covered the openings with melted wax and stacked the logs in crisscrossed layers in the woods beside the creek.

"Mushrooms like shade, but they need a bit of sunshine," says Steve. "They also like moisture, and the creek provided the perfect microclimate." By fall, they were harvesting shiitakes to sell at the farmer's market. As demand for shiitakes grew, Steve and Anne inoculated more logs. Fifteen years later they were seeding 4,000 logs with shiitake mycelium and harvesting 40 pounds (18 kg) a week. They also began growing oyster mushrooms, lions mane, and turkey tails.

Left to their own devices, shiitakes fruit twice a year, around June and August. To get a weekly harvest, Steve and Anne force their fungi to fruit by soaking logs in the creek for 24 hours. Three days later the mushrooms begin to grow.

Growing fungi outdoors produces a higher quality of mushroom, says Steve, and their taste reflects the wood they grow on. "One restaurant prefers mushrooms grown on hickory logs. Not only that, the environmental challenges they face help them develop complex flavors." Still, during a dry season, he and Anne must haul water to wet

MICROCLIMATE

A microclimate is a small, localized set of conditions that differ from the general climate. For example, cold air settling in a valley produces local frost pockets, and rivers add moisture to the surrounding air.

the logs and drape them with shade cloth.

"Our biggest challenge might be pest management," Steve says. They stack logs on gravel to discourage slugs. Deer manage to sneak a nibble now and then, "but squirrels are the toughest ones to keep out," says Steve. "They carry mushrooms up into the trees to dry out."

Truffles

Hunters with trained dogs tromp through wild undergrowth. Their clothing catches on branches and bushes as they push through cold, wet weather in search of a prize. Some days they leave the woods empty-handed. On other days, the dogs may race toward a pile of leaves, point their noses toward the ground, and begin digging into the dirt. The hunters race to the spot and gently take over digging. Their target? Truffles.

Truffles are mycorrhizal fungi, drawing sugars from plant roots and nutrients from the soil. The fruiting bodies hide among tree roots until their spores are mature. Over a million microorganisms, both bacteria and yeast, live within a truffle. Each of those tiny organisms produces chemicals which, when combined, produces the unique scent of the truffle. More than a hundred different molecules contribute to the scent of the highly coveted white truffle, *Tuber magnatum*. The potato-like truffles emit a heady scent that lures animals to them. The animals dig up the truffles, eat them, then poop, spreading the spores to new places.

Some kinds of truffles are mildly poisonous to people. Some smell terrible, and some are delicious. A small amount of truffle grated over pasta or infused into ice cream adds a deep, pungent taste and smell. The problem is that people can't find the underground truffles without help. Truffle hunters used to take pigs into the woods to locate them. But pigs love truffles too—after locating truffles, they ate them! Now truffle hunters train dogs to sniff them out.

Because they are hard to find, truffles can demand a high price. So most truffle hunters keep their collecting locations secret. They might only uncover a truffle the size of a pecan, but truffles can be

FROM THE FUNGUS FILES:
Black Truffles (*Tuber melanosporum*)

At first glance black truffles (*Tuber melanosporum*) may resemble a clump of mud, or even coal. Young oak and hazel saplings in France are often inoculated with black truffle mycelium. If conditions are right, truffles may form below the surface or among leaf litter. Inside the crusty lump is a blackish-purple and white marbled interior.

The black truffle (*Tuber melanosporum*) is a prized delicacy found in parts of Italy, France, and Spain.
Daieuxetdailleurs/Wikimedia Commons

much larger. The price of truffles depends on the type, quantity, availability, and size. One white truffle (*Tuber magnatum*) that weighed about 3.3 lbs (1.5 kg), the size of a small cantaloupe, sold for about $231,000.

Another reason truffles cost so much—several thousand dollars per pound—is because they don't last long once they're harvested. The unique aroma that makes truffles a delicacy lasts only two to three days. Experts have developed elaborate procedures to keep truffles chilled and protected so they can ship these tasty treats around the world.

Baking with Yeast

Thin or thick, the best pizza crust starts with good dough. And that dough needs yeast to rise. Yeast is a single-celled fungus known as *Saccharomyces cerevisiae*. When bakers mix the yeast with water, flour, and other ingredients, the yeast goes to work on the sugars. It digests the sugars, converting them into carbon dioxide that makes the dough rise.

It's not just pizza—bagels, pretzels, and bread depend on yeast for leavening too. Historians believe that the ancient Egyptians were the first people to realize that dough would rise if it sat around for several

Baker's yeast (*Saccharomyces cerevisiae*) reproducing through budding, magnified through scanning electron microscopy.
Mogana Das Murtey and Patchamuthu Ramasamy/ Wikimedia Commons

hours before baking. Did they know that microscopic yeasts were responsible for fluffy bread? Probably not. It wasn't until 1857 that French scientist Louis Pasteur confirmed that yeast is responsible for alcoholic fermentation.

A related yeast called *Saccharomyces exiguus* gives sourdough bread its unique flavor. Rather than adding packaged baker's yeast granules, bakers use a sourdough starter. They reserve a chunk of dough from the loaf they're making and add it to their next batch of bread, thereby ensuring the

right yeast is in the dough, giving the bread a consistent flavor.

No Fungi, No Chocolate

Have you ever seen mold growing on a piece of bread or fruit? Most fresh foods spoil quickly if not preserved. One way to preserve food is to ferment it—a technique that has been used for thousands of years. Microbes such as yeasts, molds, and bacteria release enzymes to break down the cellular structure of the food. The enzymes produced during fermentation often enhance the nutrition and keep the food from spoiling. Sometimes bacteria receive all the credit for fermentation, but without fungi, there'd be no chocolate!

A chocolate bar begins as a fat, football-shaped cacao pod. Cut it open and you'll find whitish pulp containing the cacao beans. Before those bitter beans become chocolate, they need to ferment. Fortunately, the fungi needed for fermentation are already present on the cacao pods. Workers pile the pulp-covered beans into shallow boxes and let the microorganisms get to work.

Yeast begins by fermenting the pulp, breaking down the sugars. The fermentation triggers chemical changes that give the

Make Your Own Yeast

There are more than 1,000 species of yeasts living in the natural environment. Many of them live on grapes and other fruits. In this activity you'll grow some of these wild yeasts—but they aren't the kind you'd use for baking.

MATERIALS:

- Glass or plastic container with a wide mouth and a lid that can hold about 12–16 ounces (350–470 g) (such as an old peanut butter jar)
- ½ cup (160 g) of raisins (or other dried fruits)
- 1¼ cup (300 g) of water

1. Measure ½ cup (160 g) of raisins and pour them into a jar.

2. Add 1¼ cup (300 g) of water (about three times as much water as raisins). Add more water as needed until it's about 80 percent full of water.

3. Put the lid on the jar. Let it sit on a counter at room temperature.

4. Every day, open the lid to allow fresh air into the jar. Place the lid back on the jar and shake it two to three times a day to prevent mold from growing. You should notice more and more raisins floating to the surface each day.

5. If you see small, white mold on the surface of the water or jar, remove the mold. If you cannot remove all the mold or it smells strong when you open the lid, pour it out and start over with fresh water and dried fruit.

6. After three to seven days, you'll know your experiment is successful when all the raisins are floating and the water is bubbly. When you open the lid, you should hear the bubbles lightly fizzing!

7. **Do NOT drink your yeast water!** Pour it out and clean the jar with soap and water.

beans their chocolatey flavor. Not only that, the fungi impart flavors unique to where they live, giving chocolate from one area a sweeter or fruitier taste than chocolate from another place.

Soy sauce depends on fungal fermentation too. It is made by mixing soybeans and flour into a paste, which is then shaped into a cake-like block. Then the mold *Aspergillus oryzae* is added. After only a few days, a yellow mycelium covers the cake. Water and salt are added, as well as a bacterium, to further ferment it. Several months later, the soy sauce is squeezed out of the cake.

Some cheeses, like blue cheese, are fermented. A mold called *Penicillium roqueforti*, related to the *Penicillium* mold used to make antibiotics, is added to curds. As the mold weaves a patchwork of blue-green veins through the curd, it is preserved as a new food: cheese.

Fungi Look-Alikes

There are several types of mushrooms that appear almost identical. In some cases, one is edible while its twin is toxic. This is why even experienced mushroom hunters say, "When in doubt, throw it out!"

Mushroom foragers flock to the forests in the spring in search of the morel mushrooms, *Morchella esculenta* and similar species. They're found across three-quarters of the world among soil and leaf litter. These delicate mushrooms have honeycomb-shaped heads that range in color from light brown or gray to dark brown, almost black. The term *esculenta* in Latin means "edible," though they must be cooked to be safe. The first step to identification is cutting it down the middle from cap to stem. True morels are hollow inside. The cap is also attached to the stem.

The brain mushroom, *Gyromitra esculenta*, looks a little like a morel, but has wrinkled folds on its head. A close look should help foragers distinguish these false morels from real morels. But if the cap hasn't fully unfolded, or if the mushroom is a little older, it may fool the casual observer. The false morels contain the chemical gyromitrin, a very dangerous poison that could cause death. One way to tell the two apart is by the color of their spores. Brain mushrooms have yellowish spores, whereas the edible true morels have cream-colored spores. Making a spore print would help identify what you've collected in your harvesting basket.

That small white mushroom growing in the field may look just like the white button mushrooms that you find in grocery stores. But don't eat it. Two deadly white mushrooms, the destroying angel (*Amanita bisporigera*) and the death cap (*Amanita phalloides*), are full of amatoxin, a potentially deadly toxin. These two mushrooms

Delicious, edible morels (*Morchella esculenta*). *Drew Heath/Wikimedia Commons*

Brain mushrooms, false morels (*Gyromitra esculenta*). *Kruczy89/Wikimedia Commons*

When young, the deadly destroying angel (*Amanita bisporigera*) mushroom looks similar to other edible species. *Dan Molter/Mushroom Observer*

are related to the bright red fly agaric called *Amanita muscaria*. Its bright cap and small white warts warn people away, but it contains the same toxin as the two deadly white mushrooms. When these imposters first emerge from the ground, they may resemble small white eggs. As the cap grows, it breaks the veil and starts to look more like button mushrooms.

Foragers should consult experts and field guides to avoid getting fooled by these poisonous mushrooms. It's never safe to assume that a mushroom is edible just because it looks a little like another.

FROM THE FUNGUS FILES:
Beefsteak Fungus (*Fistulina hepatica*)

Imagine walking through the woods and spying a fungus that looks more like a slice of watermelon than a mushroom. This is the beefsteak fungus, an edible fungus usually found on the side of an oak or chestnut tree. They're wet and heavy, up to 2.5 inches  (6 cm) thick, and bleed a red liquid when sliced. Many people enjoy eating the beefsteak fungus raw, sliced up in a salad, but others prefer theirs cooked.

Beefsteak fungus (*Fistulina hepatica*). *Marjolein Tschur/Wikimedia Commons*

MUSHROOM FESTIVAL

Every year, more than 100,000 people make their way to Kennett Square, Pennsylvania, for the annual Mushroom Festival. Attractions include the national fried mushroom eating championship, a mushroom 5k run/walk past local mushroom farms, an amateur mushroom cook-off, a cute-as-a-button mushroom baby contest, and tons of mushroom munchies, cookbooks, and crafted items to buy.

Identifying Wild Mushrooms

Most gardeners grow their own fruits and vegetables because fresh food tastes great! Not only that, freshly picked food is also full of nutrients. That's one of the reasons myco-philes enjoy foraging for wild mushrooms.

Experienced mushroom hunters never eat a mushroom they can't positively identify. If you want to gather edible mushrooms, go with a knowledgeable mushroom hunter who knows the area and the mushrooms that typically grow there.

MATERIALS

🍄 Your FUNgus Journal
🍄 Mushroom field guide
🍄 Plastic knife

1. Whenever you find a mushroom, try to identify it using the field guide. Take note of as many details as possible and add them to your FUNgus Journal. Here are some details to take notes about:

- Where is the mushroom located? Is it growing alone or in a clump? Near certain trees? On a rotting log?

- Does it have a sheath or ring? Mature mushrooms may have shed the sheath, but small bits of the sheath sometimes stick to the top of the mushroom.

- Is the bottom of the mushroom attached to the stem, or does it taper into the stem?

- Does the underside of the mush-room have gills or pores?

- Does the mushroom or stem change color when lightly scratched?

2. Remove the mushroom as close to the substrate as possible. Cut through the stem or cap with a plastic knife. Does this release liquid? Does the color change? Is the stem solid or hollow?

3. (Optional) Bring some identified mush-rooms home and use them to make a spore print. (See the Make a Spore Print activity on page 21.)

These are just a few things that may help you identify a wild mushroom. Never trust an online photo search to determine whether your mushroom is edible. People posting photos online may not have enough experience to correctly identify the mushroom.

When collecting mushrooms to study, always leave some behind so that the spores can mature and spread, allowing the fungus to continue its life cycle. And remember, one of the most important rules of foraging is to never eat a mush-room without being 100 percent sure of its identification!

Plan Your Own Fungus Fest

Celebrate fungi with a backyard or neighbor-hood festival. Who knows? Maybe mushroom piñatas will become the newest trend.

1. First, decide how many people you'd like to invite. If you're only inviting family and a few friends you might be able to use your home or yard. If you want a larger event, ask an adult to help you reserve space in a public park or other venue.

2. What will people do? Choose some of your favorite activities from this book. Be sure to gather enough materials before the event so that all your guests can try them. Also, think about the space you'll be using. Are there tables where people can make a craft or do an experiment?

3. Is there a park or woods nearby for a mushroom walk?

4. Invite experts or fungi enthusiasts to share their knowledge.

5. If you make some mushroom munchies, keep in mind that some people have food allergies. Many grocery stores sell stuffed mushrooms that just need to be baked. The ingredients should be labeled on these, so baking and serving them should be safe. Be sure to post signs if your snacks contain nuts, gluten, dairy, or other allergens.

6. Even if you don't want to serve food, consider asking an adult to give a cooking demonstration with mushrooms. When people see how easy it is to cook fresh mushrooms, it could inspire them to learn more about mushrooms and eat more of them too!

5

When Fungi Go Bad

When fungi are good, they are very, very good. But when they are bad, they cause problems. They infect people, plants, animals—even other fungi!

Plants aren't totally helpless. They have some defenses against intruders, such as waxy coverings on leaves or bark. Even with these barriers, some fungi manage to get in and cause disease.

Once a fungus invades, it can damage or even kill a plant. Some fungi cause wilting, while others cause

Gray mold on grapes. *Joseph Smilanick/USDA Agricultural Research Service*

A MIND-ALTERING FUNGUS

Ergot is caused by the fungus *Claviceps purpurea*. The fungus infects rye and wheat. As it grows, it produces a large, discolored grain. The disease reduces the yield and also makes powerful chemicals. When eaten, those chemicals can cause seizures, hallucinations, spasms, and delusions. Some historians think the Salem witch trials resulted from strange behaviors due to ergot poisoning. More recently, drugs derived from ergot are used to treat migraine headaches.

Ergot fungus growing from rye grain. *Dominique Jacquin/Wikimedia Commons*

In 1921 a young Dutch researcher, Marie Beatrice (Bea) Schol-Schwarz, discovered the fungus that was killing elm trees. That's how it became known as Dutch elm disease.

blotches, scabs, or rotting plant tissue. Plant-attacking fungi are sneaky. Spores sail through the air and land on the leaves, or are splashed by raindrops from one plant to another. Some fungi live in the soil, pushing their way into plants through the roots. And some spores stick to insects, hitching rides to uninfected plants.

Elm trees once lined city streets throughout the United States and Europe.

But in the 1920s, the trees began wilting and dying. The cause: an **invasive** fungus, *Ophiostoma ulmi*.

Bark beetle adults, emerging from infected trees, carried fungal spores stuck to their hard shells. Upon reaching a healthy tree, the beetles began gnawing their way to fresh, tasty bark. Fungal spores fell off or were scraped off as the beetles worked their way into the tree.

Once inside the tree, fungal spores were carried up through vascular tissue along with the flow of water. The tubes and specialized cells in the vascular system allow the tree to circulate water and minerals between its roots and leaves. To stop the infection, the tree produced a growth of cells to plug up the vascular tubes. But that also prevented water from flowing to leaves, resulting in wilt. Other fungal spores developed, sending their hyphae down into the roots. Once underground, the disease spread through root connections between nearby trees.

Dutch elm disease still affects our trees. But scientists are breeding new kinds of elm trees that are resistant to the fungus.

Rusty Grains

Fungi are the primary cause of crop loss around the world. Some destroy entire plants. Others reduce a plant's rate of photosynthesis.

Rust fungi are among the most damaging threats to crops. They don't kill their hosts, but they reduce the amount of grain harvested. There are about 7,000 species of rust fungi infecting wheat, barley, oats, soybeans, and even coffee plants. Each year wheat farmers lose more than 15 million tons of their crop to rust diseases. That's equivalent to losing nearly $3 billion a year.

The disease looks just the way you'd expect: orange to reddish blistery bumps spread over leaves and stems. The fungus produces spores inside those lumps. Blowing wind spreads spores to new plants over the growing season. Some rust fungi require an alternate host to complete their life cycles. When wheat season is over, they infect other plants including barberry, meadow rue, and clematis.

FLIGHT PLAN TO CATCH FUNGUS SPORES

Cambridge University mycologist Dillon Weston thought wheat rust spores might travel long distances on air currents. To test his theories, he needed to get into the air. He also needed a way to trap spores.

Making spore traps was the easy part. Weston smeared petroleum jelly on petri dishes. Getting into the sky was more difficult. The British Airship R100 planned to make its first transatlantic flight in July 1930, but Weston wasn't allowed to ride on the airship. Instead, the pilot agreed to collect the samples. When he reached an altitude of 2,000 feet (610 m) above the sea, the pilot held the petri dish out the window for five minutes. Brrrr!

Though Weston found rust spores in his samples, he was never able to repeat the experiment, so he never published his study.

Wheat leaves infected by wheat rust fungus. *Photo courtesy of USDA Agricultural Research Service*

Cook a Corn Mushroom Taco

If you're looking for something adventurous to eat, try this easy-to-make taco filling.

ADULT SUPERVISION REQUIRED

INGREDIENTS

- 🍄 1 tbsp cooking oil
- 🍄 ¼ small onion, diced finely
- 🍄 1 clove garlic, minced
- 🍄 1 large tomato, chopped
- 🍄 Small amount of green bell pepper or cubanelle pepper, chopped (optional)
- 🍄 6 oz (170 g) huitlacoche
- 🍄 1 or 2 leaves of epazote or sprigs of cilantro, chopped
- 🍄 4 corn tortillas
- 🍄 Salsa, for serving (optional)

1. Add cooking oil to a skillet over medium heat.

2. Add the onions and garlic and sauté for a couple minutes, until the onions are transparent.

3. Add tomato (and peppers if you want) and cook for five minutes. Stir often. The tomatoes will probably change color and start to get mushy.

4. Add the huitlacoche and epazote (or cilantro) to the frying pan. Fungi have lots of water, so the huitlacoche will release liquid. Stir over medium heat for about five more minutes.

5. Put two tablespoons of the mix into each tortilla and serve with salsa.

An ear of corn infected with smut. *Jamain/Wikimedia Commons*

Smut

Corn plants fight off more kinds of fungi than you can count on one hand. One of them is the smut fungus *Ustilago maydis*. Smut spores blow on the wind, landing on ears, leaves, and stems of corn plants. As the fungus grows, it forms swellings, called galls. Some galls are fleshy and smooth, turning black as they age. If you shuck an ear of corn and find large, grayish galls instead of sweet yellow kernels, you have smut. Some people pay good money for smut fungus.

Smut is called *huitlacoche* (whee-tla-KO-cheh) and also "corn mushroom." People in central Mexico have been frying the fungus for the past 500 years. These fat, round mushrooms contain lysine, an amino acid that helps build bone and muscle. They also have more cholesterol-reducing chemicals than oatmeal. People fill tacos with huitlacoche, toss it fresh into salads, mix it with steamed corn and zucchini, and even stir it into mac-and-cheese.

Blight, Rot, and Mummies

Tomatoes and potatoes have two types of blight to fight. Early blight is caused by the fungus *Alternaria solani*. It begins as irregular black or brown spots on the leaves. As these spots grow larger, they leave a series of rings that look like a bulls-eye. Eventually the leaves turn brown and die. Infected tomatoes begin rotting near the stem end of the fruit. In the case of potatoes, early blight causes dark, sunken spots on the skin. If you cut the potato open, you'd find dark tissue that feels a bit like cork.

You might have seen fungi on the leaves, flowers, and fruits in your own garden. Powdery mildew is a common disease and looks like white chalky spots on leaves. The disease affects a wide variety of plants, from beans and cucumbers to phlox and bee balm. Fortunately, it is host specific, which means the fungus that causes powdery mildew on grapes won't infect roses. Another fungal fruit disease is gray mold, which covers strawberries and raspberries with a fuzzy blanket. And then there's the

Severe powdery mildew on a zinnia. *Stephen Ausmus/USDA Agricultural Research Service*

Make Your Own Fungus-Fighting Mix

A fungicide is a pesticide that kills fungi or prevents them from growing. But many pesticides include chemicals that are harmful to people and pets. What's a gardener to do when fungi attack? Some use nontoxic ingredients to give their plants a fighting chance.

Here's one garden-tested, fungus-fighting formula you can make to fight powdery mildew.

MATERIALS
- Spray bottle
- Measuring spoons
- Baking soda
- Vegetable oil
- Liquid soap (Dr. Bronners or Ivory)
- Pencil
- Your FUNgus Journal

1. Pour 1 quart (1 L) of water into your spray bottle. Add 1 teaspoon (5 mL) baking soda and shake until it dissolves.

2. Add 1 teaspoon (5 mL) vegetable oil. This will help the spray to stick to leaves.

3. Add a couple drops of liquid soap. This will help keep everything mixed together.

4. Shake the mix. Spray plants early in the day, or on cloudy days. Spray tops and bottoms of leaves. Baking soda creates an environment that powdery mildew and blight fungi don't like.

5. Record your spraying schedule in your journal. Is there a noticeable change in powdery mildew or blight on the leaves?

mummy berry fungus. It shrivels blueberries into hard, black "mummies."

Crop scientists are always looking for better ways to fight crop disease. Scientists seeking a less toxic alternative to chemicals have been testing milk sprays on the powdery mildew fungus that attacks zucchini squash. They aren't sure exactly how milk works against the fungus but think it might have something to do with the protein in the milk. One of the questions researchers are trying to answer is how much milk they need for an effective spray. Is two parts milk to three parts water just as good as a 50-50 mix?

Foot and Lung Diseases

There are only about 300 species of fungus that attack humans, but they sure cause lots of problems! The most common fungal diseases are only skin deep and include nail infections, thrush, ringworm, and athlete's foot.

Nail infections are caused by yeasts and other fungi that invade through cracks in the nail or skin surrounding the nail. Thrush is also caused by a yeast that lives on the skin, though normally it doesn't cause problems. But sometimes illness, stress, or medications change the body's

THE IRISH POTATO FAMINE

In 1845, Irish potato fields were infected with late blight. The culprit: a microscopic fungus-like water mold, *Phytophthora infestans*. Because the farmers planted only one type of potato, blight spread quickly from one field to the next. The cool, damp weather contributed to the spread. Potato plants and tubers rotted in a matter of days. Irish farmers, dependent on potatoes to feed their families, lost more than half their crop. By the end of the famine in 1852, about one million people had died from starvation.

Late blight may look like a fungal disease, but *P. infestans* isn't a fungus. It is more closely related to algae and green plants.

immune balance, allowing the fungus to flourish as white patches develop and grow in the mouth and throat.

Ringworm forms itchy, ring-shaped rashes. Depending on where it grows, you might call it athlete's foot or jock itch. About 40 different fungi cause ringworm, and if there's one thing they like, it's a damp, warm place. That's why it's a good idea to wear shower shoes to the public pool and to keep your skin clean and dry.

Some fungal spores can cause respiratory diseases. Valley fever is caused by spores from the fungus *Coccidioides*. The fungus lives in the dry soil of the southwestern United States and Mexico, though recently it has been found in south-central Washington. Human activity, wind, even animals walking across the soil, can send dust and spores into the air. Most people who breathe in the spores don't get sick. Those who do can develop a cough and fever as well as fatigue, headaches, and sometimes a rash. Fortunately, people who get sick with valley fever usually get better on their own.

Don't think moving to a damp, forested region will isolate you from fungal diseases. The fungus *Blastomyces dermatitidis* hangs out in the moist soil and decomposing leaves of the Ohio and Mississippi River valleys and surrounding regions. Symptoms of blastomycosis look like other lung infections. What makes these fungal

Mushroom Stamp Art

This is a perfect way to use old mushrooms from the fridge—or any mushroom you find. You can use every part of the mushroom to make stamp art.

MATERIALS

- Mushrooms
- Knife
- Acrylic paint
- Paint brush
- Paper, card stock, brown paper bags, or newsprint
- Plastic knife or toothpick

How to make mushroom gill prints:

1. Cut the stem as close to the gills as you can.

2. Paint the underside of the mushroom, where the gills are.

3. Press the gills down onto the paper. Carefully lift off the mushroom.

How to make mushroom cap prints:

1. Cut the top half of the mushroom cap off.

2. Carve a design into the flat cap with a plastic knife or toothpick.

3. Gently brush paint across the cap, trying not to get paint into the carved design.

4. Hold the stem and press the cap onto the paper. When you lift the mushroom from the paper, you should see your unpainted design surrounded by color.

How to make textured mushroom prints:

1. Collect mushrooms with nubby caps or other textures, such as morels.

2. Brush paint on the fruit body.

3. Press or roll it onto your paper.

How to make stem prints:

1. Slice the stem across the bottom.

2. Paint the bottom of the stem and use it as a stamp.

diseases more serious than the average respiratory infection is that in some cases, the infection can spread from the lungs into the brain, spinal cord, bones, and joints.

Zombie-Making Fungi

Have you ever encountered a fly stuck to your window? Maybe you've seen a white halo around it. If so, you've met a zombie! Not too long before, this fly was buzzing around pestering people and lapping up juices from decaying fruits—or something even more disgusting. Unbeknownst to the fly, a spore from the fungus *Entomophthora muscae* landed on it. The fungus used enzymes to cut its way through the tough exoskeleton of the fly. Then the hyphae began growing inside the fly's body, digesting its guts and finally reaching its brain.

Scientists aren't exactly sure how it happens, but the fungus forces the fly to climb up a window screen or a plant stem. The last thing the fly does before it dies is grab on and spread its wings. Fuzzy white stalks push through the fly's abdomen. A single spore shoots from the end of each stalk. It's the perfect way to infect new flies!

There are hundreds of **entomopathogenic** fungi, but they each attack a specific insect. Based on ant fossils, scientists think

FROM THE FUNGUS FILES:
Scarlet Caterpillar Club (*Cordyceps militaris*)

The scarlet caterpillar club fungus infects larvae of moths and butterflies during their final stage of development in the soil. It mummifies the pupa, keeping it alive as the fungus sucks out the nutrition it needs. When the fungus is ready to fruit, it kills the insect. Then it shoots a bright orange club up through the soil to disperse its spores.

The club isn't very big—less than 3 inches (8 cm) high and about as wide as a pencil. If you see thin orange clubs growing out of grass or leaf litter, gently dig underneath them and you might find the parasitized insect! This body-snatching fungus can be found in most of North America, but it grows more densely east of the Rocky Mountains. Look for it in the summer and fall.

Scarlet caterpillar club fungus infects insects at ground level.
Andreas Kunze/Wikimedia Commons

zombifying fungi have been on the planet for the past 48 million years. Fortunately, they don't infect humans—at least not yet.

The cool thing about the insect-destroying fungi is that they all treat their hosts a bit differently. Some fungi look like a mass of fuzzy threads but the *Cordyceps* fungi produce long club-like stalks from the insects they attack. There are more than 600 species of *Cordyceps* infecting beetles, butterflies, moths, ants, and wasps. Some force their insect hosts to climb, while others attack larvae and pupae above and below the soil.

"Entomopathogenic" looks like a long, scary word. But it's not nearly as scary as becoming a zombie. Here's how you say it: EN-toe-muh-PATH-oh-GEN-ick. It means something that acts as a parasite or kills insects.

FROM THE FUNGUS FILES:
Lobster Mushroom (*Hypomyces lactifluorum*)

Despite its name, the lobster mushroom is not a fungus that grows on lobsters. It's not even a mushroom! It's a parasite. This ascomycete fungus usually overtakes basidiomycete mushrooms. It's a bit like fungus cannibalism. As the lobster fungus grows, it forms a crusty, orange shell over the host mushroom. Together, parasite and host are called a "lobster mushroom." When you cut it open, you'll find the flesh of the original mushroom on the inside. Not only does this unlikely partnership look like a lobster tail, some people think it even tastes a little like seafood!

A lobster mushroom is a parasitic fungus that grows on other mushrooms.
Alan Rockefeller/Mushroom Observer

A goldenrod soldier beetle clamps onto a flower before it dies and releases spores to infect other beetles. *Courtesy of Donald C. Steinkraus*

We're Going on a Zombie Hunt

There may be zombie insects in your backyard—or even hanging on to your window screens. Unless you are looking for them, you might not even recognize them.

MATERIALS:

- Hand lens
- Your FUNgus Journal
- Pencil
- Camera
- Colored pencils

1. Take a good look at all the window screens around your home. Do you see any flies surrounded by white powder clinging to the screen? If so, those flies were infected by *Entomophthora muscae* and the fungus has released its spores. Use your hand lens to look closely at the fly's abdomen—you may see some fungus between the segments.

2. In a garden or yard, look for dead insects clinging to the tops of stems or leaves. You may see fungal filaments or white powder around them.

3. If you find a zombie bug, write down where you found it. You might find zombie bugs on window screens, on plants, on rocks, or buried in soil, like *Cordyceps*. Take photos or draw pictures for your gallery of zombies.

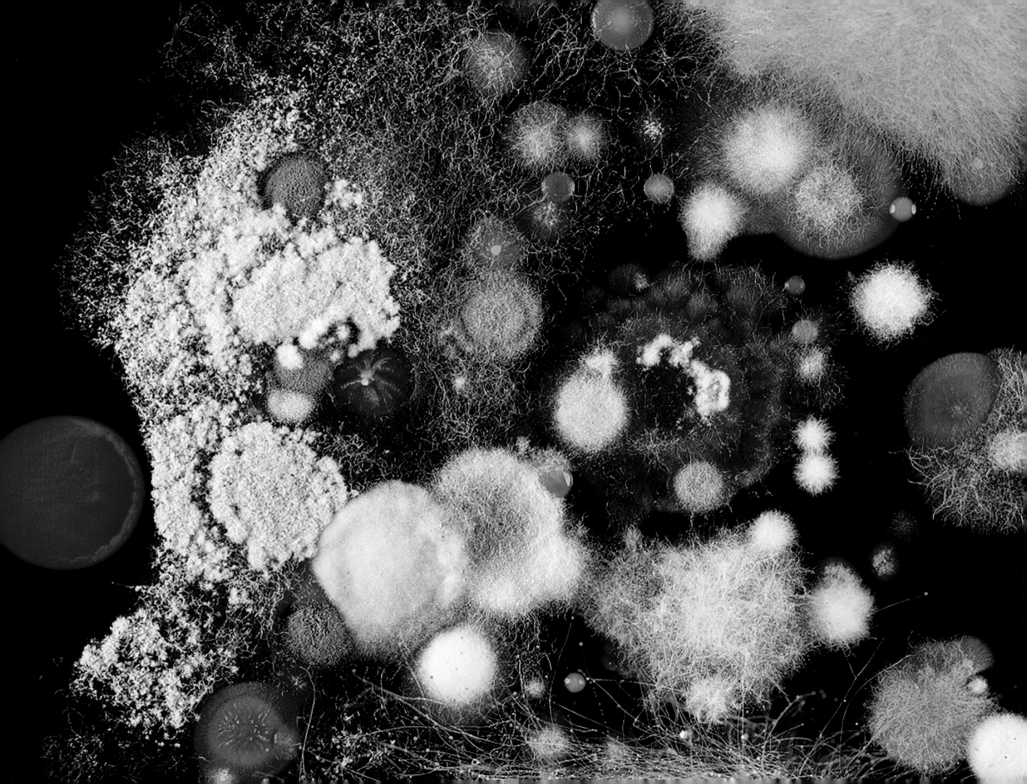

6
The Fungal Pharmacy

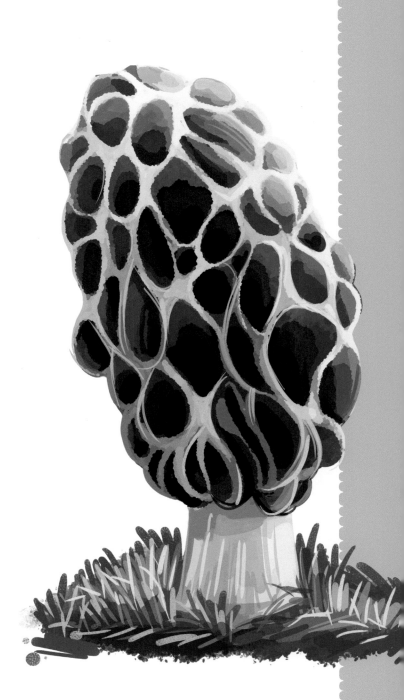

ome fungi, or the chemicals in them, are used to make medicines. Doctors use these medicines to treat patients with bacterial and fungal infections, parasites, high cholesterol, and cancer, and also to help with organ transplants. Although humans have been using fungi for healing since the time of the Neanderthals, around 130,000 to 40,000 years ago, it wasn't until the twentieth century that scientists began extracting fungal compounds for medical use.

Fungi grown from a soil sample mailed from a citizen scientist in Missouri to the Citizen Science Soil Collection Program. *Courtesy of the University of Oklahoma Citizen Science Soil Collection Program*

Penicillin: From Mold to Antibiotic

Sir Alexander Fleming usually gets the credit for discovering penicillin in 1928. It turns out that a young French doctor, Ernest A. C. Duchesne, had been experimenting with *Penicillium* strains 30 years earlier. He infected guinea pigs with different types of bacteria. Then he injected some of them with a broth containing *Penicillium glaucum* and others with saline, which is

Sir Alexander Fleming. *Wellcome Collection*

salty water. Most of the guinea pigs injected with the *Penicillium* broth survived, but those injected with saline did not. Unfortunately, Duchesne had to abandon his research when he joined the army, so no one paid much attention to his experiment.

Three decades later, Sir Alexander Fleming worked as a medical bacteriologist at St. Mary's Hospital Medical School in London. He had already discovered a bacteria-killing enzyme called lysozyme. Found in tears, saliva, and egg whites, lysozyme damages or kills bacteria by destroying their cell walls. So when Fleming noticed mold growing on one of his cultures of *Staphylococcus* bacteria, he took a closer look. The mold grew near one edge of the culture plate. It seemed to be pushing the bacteria away! Not only that, the bacterial growth closest to the mold was clear and looked like it was dissolving. Fleming realized this accidental mold could be important and began experimenting with it, calling it "mould juice." Taking a closer look, he and a colleague identified the mold as a strain of *Penicillium*.

The penicillin mold usually looks like a dark gray-green mat. As the mold grows, the surface looks like soft felt. Tiny yellow drops that resemble dew on grass appear on the surface of the mold. That's the chemical

we call penicillin. The mold produces penicillin to fight off competing microorganisms such as other fungi, bacteria, and amoebae. The penicillin also promotes symbiosis with other organisms and provides a safer environment for new spores.

When Fleming made this discovery, scientists knew that some microorganisms produced substances that kept other microorganisms from reproducing, or spreading. Fleming performed many experiments with penicillin, but he did not carry out clinical trials on animals or people. He never injected it into patients, but he did use it as an antiseptic when dressing wounds to keep bacteria from growing.

Fleming wasn't the only one doing experiments with penicillin. Over the next 10 years, a number of scientists tried, and failed, to isolate and purify its antibacterial substance. In 1932, the chemist Harold Raistrick used a penicillin broth to treat five patients with eye infections. It saved the eyesight in four of the five patients. Others used penicillin broths to treat nasal infections, eye infections, and postamputation infection with less success. Modern methods for analyzing and isolating organic compounds hadn't been invented yet. Developing penicillin into a useable drug was further slowed by a lack of funding and

Design a Postage Stamp

Many countries feature fungi on their postage stamps. Most of the images are hand drawn by artists and include the scientific name of the fungus. In this activity you will design your own pretend postage stamp.

MATERIALS

- Your FUNgus Journal or drawing paper
- Ruler
- Pencil
- Colored pencils, markers, crayons

1. Choose a type of mushroom that grows in your state or country.

2. Decide if your stamp will be horizontal or vertical. Use the ruler to help you draw the shape of your stamp. Make the stamp large enough so you can comfortably draw your design.

3. Plan your stamp design. In addition to the mushroom, you'll want to consider where to write the name of the species, the price of the postage, and even the name of the country. Look at some of the stamps in the photo to get ideas.

4. Check your field guide for ideas of what would grow around your mushroom and add those background elements to your drafts.

5. Add details to your stamp, including color.

6. Finish your stamp by sketching the perforated edges around the perimeter. They will add detail to make your stamp design look more authentic.

Fungi represented on postage stamps from several countries. *Alisha Gabriel/Author Photo*

the reluctance of scientists to share their results with competitors.

About 10 years after Fleming's experiments with penicillin, Howard Florey and Ernst Chain figured out how to isolate penicillin in larger quantities. Working with the Northern Regional Research Laboratory (NRRL) in the United States, they scaled up production of penicillin. They were racing to produce large quantities of penicillin to treat soldiers fighting in World War II. But to do that, they needed more mold samples.

People from all around the world sent soil samples to the NRRL. Would their dirt contain life-saving strains of mold? During their testing, scientists learned that certain doses of penicillin kept sick animals from dying. But they also learned that it could not be used to treat everything because, over time, bacteria could become resistant to penicillin. Developing enough penicillin to test was expensive, with no guarantee that it would be worth it. But their gamble paid off.

Alexander Fleming, Howard Florey, and Ernst Chain received the Nobel Prize in Physiology or Medicine in 1945 for their life-changing work with the first antibiotic we call penicillin. Fleming told people that he never planned to revolutionize medicine by discovering the world's first antibiotic. "I did not invent penicillin," he said. "Nature did that. I only discovered it by accident."

Statins: Fungi Fight Cholesterol

You've probably heard the saying, "You are what you eat." That doesn't mean you're a chicken if you eat an egg, but the foods you eat do affect your health. Some foods, such as milk, meat, eggs, cheese, butter, and fish contain cholesterol, a fatlike substance in the cells of your body, but your liver also produces cholesterol.

There are two types of cholesterol: high-density lipoprotein (HDL) and low-density lipoprotein (LDL). Think of lipoproteins as

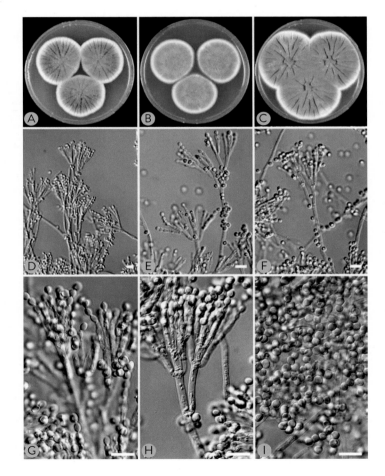

Examples of Penicillium rubens. **Samples A–C in petri dishes are seven days old and were fed different growing mediums. Examples in boxes D–H show conidiophores and box I shows conidia.**
J. Houbraken, J.C. Frisvad, and R.A. Samson/Wikimedia Commons

tiny cars driving through your blood, each carrying two passengers, protein and fat. LDL is called "bad cholesterol," because it deposits cholesterol in your arteries, like someone throwing litter out the window of the car. HDL is called "good cholesterol," because it picks up those cholesterol deposits and carries them away from the walls of your arteries. When there's too much LDL, cholesterol builds up along your artery walls, leaving less room for the blood to flow. Over time this buildup can lead to heart disease, heart attacks, and sometimes death.

Scientists have known about cholesterol for more than 250 years, but they only began studying it in the 1940s when they began looking for ways to interrupt the body's process of making cholesterol.

Inspired by Fleming's work, a biochemist named Akira Endo wondered whether a fungus might exist to help the body regulate cholesterol. He and his team tested 3,800 strains of fungi before finding a culture broth that inhibited, or lowered, the amount of cholesterol the body produced. Their tests on rats seemed promising, except that it was very bad for the kidneys. So they kept looking.

The following year they tested a mold found on rice grains. It was *Penicillium*

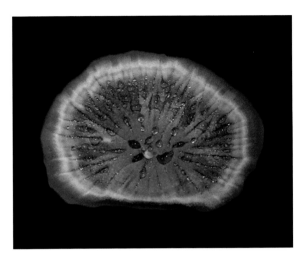

A petri dish of *Penicillium citrinum* with chemical droplets called exudate.
Courtesy of Yuri Amatnieks

citrinum, a blue-green mold similar to the one that produces penicillin. As it digests its food, this fungus produces three different **metabolic products.** Endo and his team chose to experiment with the most active one, called compactin. Their tests showed that this chemical could prevent cholesterol from forming, both in test tubes and inside living organisms. But not in rats. They tested it on other animals too, but the doses were too high. The company Endo worked for decided not to continue testing compactin.

But thanks to Dr. Endo's breakthrough research, more companies began to search for, and eventually found, fungi that

produced chemicals similar to compactin. Although Dr. Endo began his research in 1971, the first statin approved by the Food and Drug Administration (FDA) did not become available until 1987. Now, millions of people around the world take statins and live longer, healthier lives because of it.

From Fungus to Drug, a Long Process

Researchers regularly test soil samples for new fungi that can be used in medicine. They isolate each sample and analyze its DNA. This helps mycologists identify the fungus and determine whether it has been studied before. Then they grow a small amount of the fungus and extract **metabolites**. Researchers test how the metabolites act against various diseases, including cancer, infections, and diabetes.

When results seem promising, they grow large amounts of the fungus in order to produce enough metabolites for more tests. Testing usually begins in petri dishes or test tubes. The next step is animal testing, sometimes called preclinical testing. Only the most promising compounds make it this far. Later, they test the drug on a small group of healthy people, monitoring them closely for any side effects. If this trial goes well, a small number of patients with the targeted disease are given the new drug.

Pharmaceutical companies need to show that their new drug is safe and effective without bad side effects before applying to the FDA for approval to use the drug in the United States. Other countries have similar organizations that must approve drugs before they go on the market to the public. It usually takes more than 12 years to go from fungus to final drug. Even after all the testing, about 10 percent of drugs submitted for approval fall short of the rigorous standards and never make it to the public.

TRY THIS!

Do Mushrooms Absorb Water?

Some people believe that mushrooms shouldn't be washed, only wiped off with a dry or damp paper towel. They think mushrooms soak up water and will hold onto too much of it when it's time to cook them. This experiment puts that claim to the test.

ADULT SUPERVISION REQUIRED

MATERIALS

- 2 cups (150 g) white mushrooms
- Paper towels
- Cooking scale
- FUNgus Journal
- Kitchen knife
- Skillet

1. Weigh 1 cup (75 g) mushrooms and wipe them off with a dry paper towel. Set them aside.

2. Weigh the other cup of mushrooms and rinse them under running water for a few seconds to wash off any dirt. Pat them dry with a paper towel.

3. Weigh the mushrooms you just rinsed. Record their current weight in your FUNgus journal. Has it changed?

4. Ask for help from an adult to slice and cook the mushrooms. If you have two similar skillets, you may cook both groups of mushrooms at the same time. If you only have one skillet, cook the first batch of mushrooms on medium heat until they are done. Weigh them and record your results. Then cook the second batch of mushrooms the same way and for the same amount of time as the first batch. Weigh them and record your results.

5. Compare your results. Did the washed mushrooms retain water before and after cooking?

6. Taste the cooked mushrooms from both batches. Is there a noticeable difference?

Cyclosporine: Fungi Makes the Transplanted Heart Grow Fonder

In 1954, twin brothers Ronald and Richard Herrick were rolled into surgery at a hospital in Boston, Massachusetts. Doctors removed one of Ronald's kidneys and transplanted it into Richard's body. It was a success! This was the first successful human organ transplant. Doctors tried transplanting other organs: liver, heart, and pancreas. But the transplants didn't always work. Even when family members donated an organ, the patient's immune system often attacked it, recognizing it as a foreign object.

Researchers began searching for a drug that would suppress, or stop, the immune system from rejecting a new organ. They were looking for something that would stop the lymphocytes from attacking the transplanted organ. But the first immunosuppressant drugs, developed in the early 1960s, destroyed all the cells in a patient's body that divided quickly. Scientists thought that they might be able to harness the natural compounds produced by microorganisms—if only they could find the right one.

In 1969, when Hans Peter Frey returned from a vacation to Norway he brought back

FROM THE FUNGUS FILES: Lion's Mane Mushrooms

Are those icicles hanging from the side of a dead tree? No, that's *Hericium erinaceus*, also called lion's mane. The best time to find them is in the fall in the northern United States or Canada, as well as parts of Europe and Asia. When you cook up these delicious mushrooms, they might taste a little like lobster or shrimp. Many people are

interested in the health benefits of lion's mane because studies show it stimulates nerves to regrow. It's possible that compounds from lion's mane may lead to treatments for Alzheimer's disease, cancer, or helping the immune system.

The lion's mane mushroom (*Hericium erinaceus*) looks like a shaggy beard. *Lebrac/Wikimedia Commons*

a scoop of soil in a plastic bag. It wasn't unusual for scientists to scrape up soil samples—in fact, the company he worked for encouraged it. They knew that soil often contained potential drug-producing microorganisms. And in Frey's sample they found a new fungus, *Tolypocladium inflatum gams*.

They started out testing it for use as an antibiotic. The research team separated two metabolites they called cyclosporine

A and B, which failed. Cyclosporine wasn't useful as an antibiotic. But given its low level of toxicity, the scientists wondered whether it could be used in another type of medicine?

Meanwhile, another scientist at the company, Jean-François Borel, had his own ideas about testing chemicals for immune suppression drugs. When they applied his ideas to cyclosporine, the tests revealed its potential as an immune suppressant.

Now testing began in earnest. Scientists injected foreign cells into mice. Then some of the mice received doses of cyclosporine. A few days later, researchers tested the mice's blood. The mice that were given cyclosporine had not developed antibodies to fight off the foreign cells.

Another test showed that while cyclosporine inhibited antibody development, it didn't suppress all cell growth and division. That's important, because some of your body's systems are constantly creating new cells, such as your bone marrow. A drug that can target your immune system is better than one that suppresses all cell growth.

Because organ transplants were rarely done, the company decided it was too expensive to continue researching cyclosporine as an immunosuppressant. But some of the scientists on the team didn't want to give up. They wondered whether the drug could be used for other purposes, such as fighting inflammation. Microbiologists grew more of the fungus and the researchers tested cyclosporine on more animals.

When David J. G. White learned of cyclosporine, he requested a sample to test with animal transplant experiments at Cambridge University. Two years later, in 1978, cyclosporine was given to a patient to help their body accept a kidney transplant.

The Cambridge animal studies helped to convince the pharmaceutical company to begin clinical trials. Scientists in several countries requested samples of cyclosporine in its raw form to run their own experiments. Eventually, cyclosporine was approved by the FDA. Today, it is commonly used as a posttransplant treatment.

Fighting Cancer

The first record of using mushrooms to treat illness was written 5,000 years ago.

FROM THE FUNGUS FILES:
Caterpillar Fungus (*Ophiocordyceps sinensis*)

High up in the Himalayas on the Tibetan Plateau, men, women, and children bend down and peer carefully at the grassy meadow. They're looking for a brownish stalk sticking up among the grasses. It's not a plant, though. It's the stalk of the fungus *Ophiocordyceps sinensis*, called "winter worm-summer grass" by the locals. Like the scarlet caterpillar club, this fungus grows from the body of an insect, the ghost moth caterpillar. When one of the gatherers finds one, they carefully dig into the ground around it, trying not to break the fungus stalk.

Caterpillar fungus has been harvested and used in traditional Chinese medicine for at least 500 years. Some people use it to improve their immune system, helping them avoid illness or recover from sickness. Others use it to treat anemia, pain, coughing, tuberculosis, and even cancer. Modern researchers have begun studying the compounds produced by the fungus. One promising thread of their research may lead to a drug to manage diabetes.

Two ghost moth caterpillars overtaken by the fungus *Ophiocordyceps sinensis*. The stalk of the fungus is still attached to one caterpillar. *L. Shyamal/Wikimedia Commons*

FROM THE FUNGUS FILES:
Reishi, *Ganoderma lucidum*

Ganoderma lucidum, or reishi, is also nicknamed the lacquered bracket because of its hard, shiny appearance. It's a common mushroom found in Europe and parts of China that is often dried and added to tea. Many people take reishi

when combating cancer and liver diseases, and it has been used as a supplement in Asia for a long time. Active substances called triterpenoids and polysaccharides in reishi are being studied in China to treat lung cancer and in Japan to treat colon cancer.

Reishi (*Ganoderma lucidum*) is a bracket fungus that grows on trees.
Dave Ross/Mushroom Observer

MARINE FUNGI AS A TREATMENT FOR CANCER

Researchers are studying metabolites from a wide variety of marine fungi in their search to develop new drugs to treat cancer. Marine fungi appear to have more diverse chemicals than fungi found on land. This might be explained by their range of habitats, from sediments deep below the surface to those living in sponges, causing them to develop different metabolites. So far, scientists have isolated 1,000 unique metabolites from marine fungi that could lead to future drugs.

People in different parts of the world have written about mushroom medicine since then, but it is in China that medical mushroom use thrives, especially to treat cancer. There are over 100 known mushrooms used in Asia to treat cancer.

One medicinal fungus is the common turkey tail, *Trametes versicolor*. It grows on dead logs, fanning out in beautiful rings of browns and tans and other colors. People brew it as a tea or swallow it in a capsule to strengthen the immune system, especially when treating cancer. The reason: turkey tail mushrooms produce a compound called polysaccharide-K, or PSK for short. It had long been used as a traditional immunity booster, but in the 1960s, researchers in Japan began testing the anticancer properties of PSK. In clinical trials, cancer patients who took PSK along with their other treatments produced more cancer-killing cells. Not only was their cancer less likely to return, they lived longer. Although the FDA has not approved PSK as a medication, people can buy it over the counter just like vitamins.

Shiitake mushrooms (*Lentinula edodes*) provide another promising cancer treatment. Many people eat them as part of their diet, but these fungi may also benefit health. Lentinan, a sugar molecule found in the mushrooms, may boost the immune system, thereby helping to fight cancer.

Just as researchers looked for specific compounds in fungi to create antibiotics, statins, and immunosuppressants, many

Lobby for a State Fungus

All 50 states in the United States have named official state flowers, trees, mammals, and birds, but only Minnesota, Oregon, and Texas have designated a state fungus. Minnesota picked the morel mushroom (Morchella esculenta) *as its state fungus in 1984. Oregon chose the Pacific Golden Chanterelle* (Cantharellus formosus), *another tasty mushroom, in 1999. Texas designated* Chorioactis geaster, *a star-shaped fungus that is only found in Texas and Japan, as the state mushroom in 2021.*

Golden Chanterelle (*Catharellus formosus*). *Ron Pastorino/Mushroom Observer*

If your state has not designated a state fungus, perhaps it's time to lobby for one! Here's how to get started:

1. Use a field guide to identify mushroom species that grow in your area.

2. Choose a type of mushroom from your area and list two or three reasons why you think it would be a good choice as a state mushroom, for example, it's beautiful, edible, rare, or only grows in your area.

3. Contact a local or state mycological society. Tell them your idea for naming a state mushroom and ask for their support.

4. Write to your state representatives and ask them to sponsor legislation to name your chosen mushroom as the state mushroom. Be sure to list your reasons, and if possible, include a photo.

researchers hope to find the right compounds from fungi to counteract cancer. It is very complicated, though. There are many types of cancer and numerous ways to approach treatments. That is why current studies focus on the compounds found in fungi as well as the way combining fungal extracts can affect cancerous tumors. Until prescription cancer drugs are developed and available to the public, many people will likely continue turning directly to mushrooms—to these and other mushroom supplements that have been used for thousands of years.

From Hallucinogenic Drugs to Modern Medicine

Psilocybin, a compond found in about 200 kinds of psilocybin mushrooms, produces hallucinogenic effects when ingested, like seeing colorful shapes swirling through your mind. It has been used for centuries in religious rituals throughout Mesoamerica and Europe.

Researchers at the University of South Florida have been studying the effects of psilocin on mice. First, the mice were taught to fear a certain sound and to expect pain each time they heard it. After being treated with psilocin, the mice didn't show signs of fear when the noise was played.

Could the mushroom chemical have changed their minds? Tests showed that the mice had experienced new nerve growth in their brains. Continuing research indicates that psilocin might help humans heal from trauma or depression and to develop healthier neural pathways. Studies also show that the correct doses of psilocin can help terminally ill patients live more peacefully, without fearing death.

Fruiting bodies of the hallucinogenic mushroom *Psilocybe semilanceata. Alan Rockefeller/ Mushroom Observer*

Follow a Fungus Friend

Have you ever stood against a wall to have your height measured? Or stepped onto a scale to check your weight? Just as people grow and change over time, so do fungi! Follow the steps in this activity to see how much the fungi in your area grow or change.

MATERIALS

- 🍄 FUNgus Journal
- 🍄 Pencil
- 🍄 Ruler
- 🍄 Camera, if available

1. Locate a mushroom, lichen, or mold in your yard or somewhere near your home or school. Hint: if you're having trouble finding one, keep in mind that even a moldy piece of fruit would make a good fungus to follow.

2. Set up a page in your journal for recording information about this fungus.

3. Either make a sketch of the fungus in your journal, or take a photo.

4. Write the date and time you first observe the fungus.

5. Measure and describe the fungus in your journal. What are the weather conditions? Write that down too.

6. Check on your fungus every day if you can. Take photos and make note of any changes you see. Has it grown? Is it plump or wrinkled? Have any insects or small animals nibbled on it?

7. Record your observations. Does the weather or time of day effect your fungus friend? Does the color stay the same each day, or change? Is there noticeable growth?

8. Follow your fungus friend for a week or more and record your observations.

7

Putting Fungi to Work

Fungi generally mind their own business—digesting dead leaves, dissolving headstones—but people have discovered that fungi can be useful partners. Investigators use fungi to help solve crimes, shippers use fungi as packing material, and farmers use fungi to help control pests. Fungi even play a role in household cleaning!

A decomposing fungus on a pumpkin, seen through a stereomicroscope.
Karl Az/Wikimedia Commons

Forensic Mycology

Imagine you're tossing a ball to a friend and it accidentally lands in your neighbor's yard. You peek through the bushes and see it. The coast is clear, so you carefully duck under a branch, tiptoe across the yard, and grab your ball. You run back toward your yard. Your pants brush against your neighbor's primroses. You stop and look down. The flowers look OK. You push your way through the bushes and make it back to your yard. Phew! Your neighbor will never know you were there. Right?

You may not see it, but you left a trail of evidence behind you. According to Locard's exchange principle, everywhere you go you leave something behind and also carry something away with you. On television and in movies, law enforcement officers often look for DNA, such as pieces of hair or fingerprint evidence to prove that someone was at a crime scene. But there are other types of evidence to tie a person to a scene, including pollen grains, bacteria, soil, parts of insects, and even fungal spores. These microscopic bits are called **palynomorphs** (pah-LEEN-uh-morfs). The people who collect and analyze them for evidence in court cases are called forensic ecologists.

When you went to retrieve your ball, your shoes would have carried microscopic materials into your neighbor's yard. When you returned to your own yard, your shoes probably picked up tiny pollen grains from the primrose flowers. And spores of a rare fungus that only grows on primrose leaves may have stuck to your clothes. Your hair trapped the microscopic evidence of your excursion, too, and particles are even trapped inside your nose!

The field of forensic ecology is relatively new, and it takes a very knowledgeable person to collect and interpret the results. Patricia Wiltshire, a forensic ecologist working in the United Kingdom, wrote, "It involves aspects of botany, of palynology (the study of pollen, spores, and other microscopic entities), mycology (the study of fungi), bacteriology, entomology (the study of insects), parasitology, human, animal, and plant anatomy, soil and sediment science, statistics, and many other 'ologies.'"

Upon reaching a crime scene, a forensic ecologist takes a variety of surface samples, such as gathering bits of soil. Each is photographed and recorded in their notes. Then back at the lab, the samples are placed in a centrifuge, which processes them into pellets. Wearing a face mask, gloves, and protective clothing, the scientist then treats the samples with strong acids to separate the palynomorphs from the soil. This process stains the palynomorphs red. The scientist mixes the palynomorphs in a special jellylike substance, spreads it on a glass slide, and places it under the lens of a microscope. Then the scientist begins to identify and count evidence such as pollen grains and fungal spores. Each particle may

LOCARD'S EXCHANGE PRINCIPLE

Edmond Locard was born in France in 1877 and studied medicine. During World War I he worked with the French secret service as a medical examiner. His job was to analyze soldiers' uniforms in order to identify the cause and location of their deaths. Locard created the first crime investigation laboratory in an attic above the Lyon police department. Locard's exchange principle is his most famous contribution to **forensic** science. It states that "every contact leaves a trace."

Grow a Mold Garden

Molds aren't as big and bold as mushrooms, but they have their own beauty.

MATERIALS

- Knife
- Leftover food: bread, fruit, vegetables (DO NOT use any food containing meat, oils, or dairy—they will get very smelly after a day or two)
- Water
- Spray bottle (optional)
- One or more clear containers with lids (large glass jars, plastic containers, even plastic take-out containers with clear lids will work, but check with an adult to make sure you can throw it away when you are finished)
- Masking tape or duct tape
- Pencils
- Camera
- FUNgus Journal

CAUTION: *Some molds are not healthy to inhale. Do not open the lid to your garden container—not even to get a closer look. When you're finished with the mold garden, throw it in the garbage. Don't reuse the container.*

1. Choose four or five pieces of food. Grapes are already the right size. Cut bigger pieces of food into chunks about an inch long.

2. Dip pieces of food into water, or spray them with a little spritz of water.

3. Place food in your container. Spread them out so they don't touch each other. If you are using a jar, think about turning it on its side. If you are using small jars, put only one or two foods in them.

4. Put the lid on your container. Tape around the edge to seal it.

5. Label your container "mold garden" so no one accidentally throws it away. Then put it in a place where no one will knock it over and where you can watch it. It doesn't need to be in the light.

6. Check your mold garden every day. It might take two or three days for mold to start growing. When it does, write down what you see. Take pictures or draw what the mold looks like. Here are some things to notice:

   - What food gets moldy first?
   - What color is the mold on each food item?
   - Is the mold fuzzy? Is it spotty?
   - Does the mold grow in a pattern, like a target?
   - Does mold spread from one food item to another?

7. After a week, food will start to rot. What happened to the mold?

8. When rot takes over (around two weeks) it's time to pitch your mold garden into the garbage. Remember: **do not open the container**—just throw it away. But first, take a final picture.

be no bigger than a speck of dust. It may seem impossible that a scientist could tell the particles apart, but every tiny grain or spore has unique characteristics.

Patricia Wiltshire, a forensic ecologist, developed many of the procedures that other forensic ecologists follow now. She starts at the top left corner of the slide and studies it section by section, identifying and counting palynomorphs. If she finds something she doesn't recognize, she labels it "unknown" and goes back to look at it again later. When a forensic ecologist stumbles across something they don't recognize, they have a few options. First, they might pull out their reference slides to try to find a match. But they can also reach out to other experts to help them identify it.

A forensic ecologist can spend hours, days, or even weeks poring over slides, comparing evidence from crime scenes to evidence taken from a suspect's clothing, shoes, or even the floor mats of their car. Then they share their findings with law enforcement, often helping them to fill in the missing clues.

Fungi Fight Stains

Would you put fungus in the washing machine with your laundry? Why not! Fungi produce a lot of powerful enzymes to break down the dead leaves, wood, and animal remains they depend on for food. It was only a matter of time until scientists discovered which enzymes could dissolve tough grease, grime, and grass stains on clothes.

In an experiment, researchers found that fungal lipases dissolved olive oil right off dirty napkins. They also discovered different enzymes that help keep colors bright, remove chocolate stains, and allow detergents to work at cooler water temperatures.

The detergent in your laundry room could contain as many as eight different enzymes. Not only do those enzymes help the environment—washing laundry in cold water uses less energy—but developing those enzymes generates billions of dollars for the labs producing them.

FROM THE FUNGUS FILES:
Oyster mushroom (*Pleurotus ostreatus*)

When oyster mushrooms get hungry, they eat dead trees by making enzymes that digest the lignin in the wood. Industrial scientists are interested in one group of these enzymes called proteases. Proteases break down proteins, which is important for removing stains in clothing. Because oyster mushrooms grow in a cool climate, the proteases they produce are active at a lower temperature. Laundry detergents based on these enzymes could clean synthetic fibers that shouldn't be washed in hot water. Not only that, this kind of laundry detergent would be biodegradable.

Oyster mushrooms not only taste good, but they can help get the stains out of your laundry. *Jerzy Opioła/Wikimedia Commons*

Once they find a useful enzyme, scientists need to produce enough for billions of bottles of laundry detergent. One way to get that much would be grinding up mushrooms and extracting the enzyme. But that would require tons of mushrooms. So instead, they study the DNA from the mushroom. When they locate the gene that produces the enzyme, they insert it into another, faster-growing organism, such as yeast. This way they can make large quantities of the enzyme and leave the fungi growing in the forest.

Down on the Farm

With so many kinds of fungi attacking crops, it seems unlikely that farmers would apply fungi to their fields on purpose. But there are plenty of beneficial fungi that can help fight plant-munching insects.

Scientists have identified around 1,000 species of entomopathogenic fungi that could be put to use. The challenge is to figure out how to mass-produce a product that farmers can apply using the machinery they already have. For many products, that means suspending spores in a liquid that can be sprayed.

The most widely used fungus in commercial biopesticides is *Beauveria bassiana*.

TRY THIS!

Write a Haiku

A haiku is a traditional Japanese poem. Haiku are short, like poetry snapshots. They are only three lines long and follow a pattern. The first line has five syllables, the second has seven, and the last has five. The lines usually don't rhyme.

Most haiku celebrate nature, and fungi make a great topic. To get started, think about what you want to say. Maybe you want to write about a mushroom in your yard. Jot down words that describe it. What observations do you want to share? Now put it together in your lines of five syllables, seven syllables, and five syllables. Then share it with your friends.

Here's an example to get you started:

> *Beneath red maples,*
> *this crusty rock invader*
> *covers old headstones.*

It attacks aphids, caterpillars, and other leaf-nibblers such as grasshoppers and Colorado potato beetles. Fungi make good **biocontrol** sprays because they usually don't affect people or other animals. But it can take as long as a week for the fungus to grow and attack the harmful insects.

An emerald ash borer infected with *Beauveria bassiana* emerges from a tree.
Houping Liu/USDA Agricultural Research Service

Because fungi are living, environmental factors can influence how well the pesticide works. Hot, dry weather can inactivate spores. Also, because they attack a broad range of insects, that means they might also attack beneficial insects such as lady beetles.

Foresters are interested in potential applications of fungal controls too. The *Beauveria* fungus used in farm fields has shown some promise in killing adult emerald ash borer beetles, an invasive species that has already killed millions of trees. Another invasive species is the caterpillar *Lymantria dispar*. This caterpillar can quickly defoliate trees. Although there is no fungal spray for caterpillars, scientists collected the fungus *Entomophaga maimaiga* from Japan in the early 1900s to use as a biological control against the moth larvae. The good news is that this fungus seems to be growing stronger in northeastern forests.

It's not just insect pests that catch the attention of scientists. There's increasing concern about herbicide-resistant weeds. Some scientists have set their sights on fungi as potential weed-control agents. Fungi have been used to control dandelions, clovers, and several other weeds. Now scientists are studying *Myrothecium*

IT'S A FUNGUS-EAT-FUNGUS WORLD

Trichoderma fungi live in nearly all soils and help promote root development by forming mycorrhizal partnerships with plants. But many species of *Trichoderma* are mycoparasites, meaning they eat other fungi. Because they live at the root zone, they help protect plants from wilts, root rots, and fungal diseases that attack the stem. *Trichoderma* also fights gray molds on strawberries and cucumbers, early blight in tomatoes and potatoes, rice blast fungus, and black spot (*Anthracnose*) on beans.

verrucaria as a biocontrol for kudzu. Kudzu plants grow at an astonishing rate of 1 foot (0.3 m) a day. The fungus works just as quickly. Researchers reported that plants sprayed with the fungus in the morning started showing signs of infection a few hours later.

Packing Material

The fruits, vegetables, and grains that you find in the grocery store are only the edible parts of the plant. What happens to the leftover stalks, stems, and other parts of the plants? Some innovative people are using fungi to transform the inedible stems, leaves, and vines into environmentally friendly products such as textiles, construction materials, furniture, and packaging materials.

If a manufacturer needs a protective package to ship their product, they might turn to a company such as Ecovative Design to create one from mycelium. The company designs a reusable plastic form to fit the

Mycelium-based product packaging made by Ecovative Design. *Courtesy of Ecovative Design*

product. Then they fill it with mycelium and hemp hurds, the chopped-up stalks of fiber hemp plants. Then they allow the mycelium to grow for a few days. Once the mycelium has covered the form, they dehydrate the packaging to be sure the mycelium stops growing. They pop the mycelium package out of the form and begin the whole process again. It only takes a week.

Products can then be packed in their custom mycelium packages and shipped to stores. When a customer gets the product home, they can compost the packaging, which breaks down in about a month. Not only is this better for the environment than Styrofoam or plastic packaging that would end up in landfills, but by composting the mushroom packaging, nutrients are returned to the soil. More and more mushroom packaging is being made for all kinds of products, but it has also inspired other mycelium-based projects.

Using Fungi in Art and Architecture

Once a decomposing fungus has attacked a piece of wood, it breaks down the lignin, making the wood softer and less dense. Sometimes it even makes the wood beautiful! Woodworkers often search for fungi-infected logs, called spalted wood, to make decorative items such as bowls, boxes, and musical instruments. Depending on the fungi, woodworkers can end up with interesting colors and designs in their wood.

One fungus creates black zigzagging lines in the wood. White rot fungi lightens, or bleaches, the color of the wood as it breaks down the lignin. And other fungi produce pigments that stain the wood blue, pink, green, or other colors. Sometimes a lucky carver finds all three types of spalting

Bowls and pens handmade from different types of spalted wood. *Alisha Gabriel/Author Photo*

FUNGAL FASHION

Designers are starting to experiment with a soft, leather-like material made from mycelium to make bags and shoes. In 2021, Adidas announced they would be incorporating mycelium-based materials into their new Stan Smith Mylo sneaker. Designers are getting more adventurous and starting to use myco-leather and thinner myco-fibers to make clothes too.

The new Stan Smith Mylo Sneaker by Adidas. *Courtesy of Adidas*

FROM THE FUNGUS FILES:
Green Elf Cup

Turquoise wood is an unusual sight in the woods. If you see it, the green elf cup fungus was almost certainly involved. Although it forms tiny greenish-blue cups no bigger than a pencil's eraser, it is actually the unseen mycelium that causes the beautiful turquoise stain of spalted wood.

This green elf cup fungus (*Chlorociboria aeruginascens*) gives spalted wood its blue-green color.
Lukas Large/Flickr

in the same piece of wood. Spalted wood is so cool that scientists and woodworkers have found ways to inoculate wood with fungi on purpose!

That's not the only way people are using fungi in art and architecture. Architects at The Living company in New York City were inspired by the mycelium packaging being made by Ecovative Design. *What else could be made with mycelium?* they wondered. *Could we make bricks?*

They needed to submit plans for an innovative structure to win the Young Architects Program competition, so they designed a three-legged tower that fed into three

chimney-like openings made of mycelium bricks. It would require 10,000 bricks and rise about 40 feet (12 m) into the sky. They even built a model and a small wall made of mycelium bricks for the competition.

They won! That meant that their project, called the Hy-Fi Tower, would be built and exhibited for three months at MoMA PS1, the Museum of Modern Art in Queens, New York.

The architects enlisted Ecovative Design to make the bricks for the tower. Ecovative's engineers started with corn stalks from local farmers. They broke the corn stalks up into smaller pieces, inoculated them

(above) **Mycelium bricks grown in plastic forms.** *Courtesy of The Living*

(left) **The Hy-Fi Tower on display in the courtyard of the Museum of Modern Art, MoMA PS1.** *Amy Barkow, Courtesy of The Living*

with mycelium, and poured the mixture into plastic forms. After about five days, the mycelium had woven around the corn stalks and filled the brick forms. Still, it took 10 weeks to grow 10,000 bricks!

Once the bricks were ready, the architects hired masons to construct the tower. The lightweight bricks and unique shape of the structure complicated the assembly, so several architects and college students stepped in to help. The lead architect, David Benjamin, said they "laid out templates and bricks and prepared string guidelines to help position everything correctly." It took about four weeks to build the tower.

When the exhibit ended, the Hy-Fi Tower was disassembled and composted, allowing nutrients to return to the soil. Benjamin said that "in the near future, mycelium material could be further engineered to create structural blocks, columns, and panels for larger and more complex buildings. . . . We are only just getting started!"

Is There Anything Fungi Can't Do?

People sometimes ask, "What can we make from fungi?" Wouldn't the better question be, "Is there anything we can't make from fungi?" Innovators have made furniture, formed panels for homes, and even built a canoe out of mycelium!

Before companies began marketing mycelium-based products, American artist Miriam C. Rice pioneered the use of mushrooms to dye fabric and yarn. She didn't stop there. She used the dense fibers of polypore mushrooms to make paper and created watercolor paints from fungi dyes. She also combined mushroom pigments with beeswax to create crayons she calls MycoStix™.

FROM THE FUNGUS FILES:
A Mushroom to Dye For (*Cortinarius semisanguineus*)

In ancient Rome, if you wanted a purple robe, you'd have to collect thousands of sea snails and boil them in a lead vat. Only the wealthiest government officials and rulers could afford the costly dye. Eventually the Roman Emperor proclaimed laws reserving purple for royalty and forbidding citizens from using the color.

Years later, dyers discovered other ways to produce the color. One way is to boil the caps of red-gilled *Cortinarius semisanguineus* mushrooms. Depending on the type

of fiber and the mordant, dyers can produce a range of colors from pinks to reds to purples. Mordant is a chemical that helps the dye soak into the fabric and keeps the color from washing out. The lead in the Roman dye vats acted as a mordant, but most home dyers use alum, copper, iron, or even vinegar.

(top) *Cortinarius semisanguineus*, a mushroom commonly used to dye fibers. *Walt Sturgeon/Mushroom Observer*

(bottom) Wool and silk fibers dyed with *Cortinarius semisanguineus*. *Courtesy of Heidi Tyrväinen*

Bundle Dye with Fungi

Bundle dyeing is a fun way to get some mushroom colors onto an old, white T-shirt, napkin, or pillowcase. Or repurpose white sheets into scarves. Make sure the fabric has been washed and well rinsed before dyeing. You will need an adult to help.

ADULT SUPERVISION REQUIRED

MATERIALS

- 🍄 Alum (find in art store or with pickling supplies)
- 🍄 ¼ cup (60mL) measuring cup
- 🍄 Fabric to dye: pillow case, T-shirt, white napkin
- 🍄 White vinegar
- 🍄 Spray bottle
- 🍄 Mushroom pieces (a good one to use is the dyer's polypore mushroom, *Phaeolus schweinitzii*. It grows across North America.)
- 🍄 Dandelions or other flower petals

- 🍄 White string or twine
- 🍄 Enamel or stainless steel pot you don't use for cooking
- 🍄 Steaming basket or colander you don't use for cooking
- 🍄 Lid to cover pot
- 🍄 Tongs
- 🍄 Scissors
- 🍄 Iron

1. Mix ¼ cup (60mL) alum for each quart (or liter) of hot water. It doesn't need to be boiling—hot from the tap will work.

2. Get your fabric wet and squeeze out the water. Then put it in the alum solution to soak overnight. This helps bind the dye to the fabric.

3. The next morning, squeeze the alum solution from the fabric. Lay the fabric out on a flat surface.

4. Pour vinegar into the spray bottle and spray the fabric. This helps keep the color after dyeing.

5. Place pieces of mushroom on the shirt. Sprinkle flower petals on, too, if you want. But leave white space for the mushroom pigments to spread.

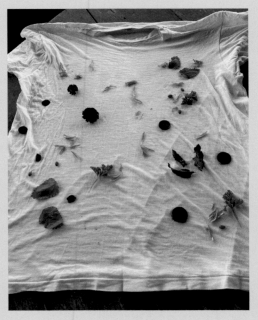

Place pieces of mushrooms along with flower petals and leaves onto your fabric.
Sue Heavenrich

6. Begin rolling the fabric from one end. When you're finished, it will look like a snake. Then start at one end and roll it like a cinnamon bun. Tie it together with string or twine.

Once the fabric is rolled and tied, the bundle is ready to place into the steamer in the dye pot. *Sue Heavenrich/Author Photo*

7. Fill the pot about one-third of the way with water and heat to boiling. Put the fabric bundle in the steamer (or colander) inside the pot and put the lid on. Let it simmer for an hour or two. Check the bundle every 20 minutes to make sure some color is bleeding through. Using tongs, turn the bundle over. After an hour, if it has a lot of color, you can stop. Otherwise, let it continue to steam.

8. When it's done, turn off the heat. Let the bundle stay in the pot to cool overnight. Leave the bundle tied up until it feels dry.

9. Take the bundle outside to unwrap. Cut the strings and unfold the fabric. Shake out the mushrooms, flower petals, or leaves. Then hang to finish any drying.

10. Iron the fabric using a steam setting to help set the colors in.

8

The Future of Fungi

Planet Earth is full of pollution and chemicals. Many corporations work to contain the dangerous chemicals or wastewater created by their industry but it's not always possible, and accidents happen as well. When farmers spray pesticides to get rid of insect pests on their crops, pesticide residue stays in the soil. Some of those chemicals dissolve in rain and wash into rivers and streams, harming fish, plants, and aquatic insects. They are also carried into

The mycelium of oyster mushrooms (*Pleurotus ostreatus*) helps break down pollutants.
Peter Stevens/Flickr

groundwater, which may provide drinking water for people. Pesticide residues also harm the insects, worms, and fungi that keep soil healthy.

Soil contaminated with chemicals or heavy metals is often dumped in landfills. Even wildfires contaminate the soil. Cleaning up contaminated soil presents a huge challenge. Fortunately, fungi come to the rescue.

Mycoremediation

On a hot, windy day in October 2017, three wildfires burned through three neighboring counties in California. They raced across 250 square miles, incinerating 6,000 homes, businesses, and open land, taking more than 20 lives.

That destruction was bad enough, but there was another danger: the ash left behind was full of toxic chemicals from the buildings and vehicles that had burned, including homes full of cleaning supplies, paints, oil, and more. Those chemicals could contaminate drinking water, farmland, and streams that spill into the Pacific Ocean!

A group of residents and specialists established the Fire Mediation Action Coalition to figure out how to stop that from happening. They had to move fast. Their first step was building about 300,000 feet, roughly 56 miles (90 km), of wattles. Wattles are straw-filled, snakelike tubes used to stop runoff and reduce erosion. Volunteers placed the wattles in important areas to help prevent erosion and the spread of toxic chemicals.

It wasn't enough, though. Winter was fast approaching, which meant lots of rain. The rain could wash toxins into drains, polluting the water system. So they decided to add a new level of defense—mushrooms.

Introducing mycelium of mushrooms to help break down or clean up pollution is called **mycoremediation**. It is a type of bioremediation, using living organisms to clean up pollutants. For the past 40 years, microbes have helped clean up oil spills, break down insecticides in soil, remove heavy metals from soil, and even eat plastic! Since 2005, scientists have been studying how they might add fungi to the bioremediation toolbox.

The coalition added oyster mushroom mycelium to the straw in as many of the wattles as possible. They chose oyster mushrooms because this fungus breaks down natural elements, such as oil and gas. Plus, their mycelia can trap metals and toxins.

That winter was dryer than expected. The mushrooms didn't receive much moisture, which limited their growth. It also meant there wasn't as much runoff from flooding. The coalition didn't have time to set up a scientific study, so they weren't sure how many toxins were trapped by the mycelium or how much might have washed into the water system. But researchers continue studying these types of mycoremediation efforts because wildfires are a constant danger. The information they glean from their studies could help communities make a plan to protect their land and water if a wildfire springs up in their area.

Other mycoremediation studies focus on pollutants that occur outside of natural disasters, and oyster mushrooms aren't the only fungi under the microscope. Certain species of fungi are able to gather and contain large quantities of arsenic, while others seem to take silver into their fruiting bodies. Though they're not sure why this happens, scientists have a few hypotheses. Gathering these elements may benefit the fungus in some way. It may help the fungus defend the fruiting bodies from predators, such as insect larvae that won't eat that particular element. Or, the fungus may not have developed the ability to filter out the elements or to get rid of them when they ingested.

Adopt an Endangered Fungus

People "adopt" tigers, elephants, and otters in conservation efforts. So why not adopt an endangered fungus? Fungi may not be furry, but they're every bit as cute—and as important—as the animals used to promote conservation awareness.

MATERIALS

- Mushroom field guide and/or online access
- Your FUNgus Journal
- Colored pencils and a pen

1. Choose an endangered fungus to learn more about. If you have access to a computer, the International Union for Conservation of Nature's Red List (www.iucnredlist.org) is a great resource.

2. Describe your fungus. Draw and color a picture of the fungus, or print out a photo to glue in your journal.

3. Where does it live? Draw a map or describe its habitat and range. If it lives near you, go on an expedition to find it.

4. Write down why this fungus is important. Why should it be saved?

5. Create an adoption certificate for your fungus.

Endangered fungi in North America

Bridgeoporus nobilissimus, found in northwest United States

Cetradonia linearis, found in the Appalachian Mountains

Cladonia perforate, found in the state of Florida

Hapalopilus croceus, found in eastern United States, also Europe and Asia

Clavaria zollingeri, found in northeastern regions of the United States

Buchwaldoboletus lignicola, found from Ontario, Canada, to Pennsylvania

Agaricus pattersoniae, found in central coastal California

Endangered fungi from around the world

Tricholoma acerbum

Hydnellum mirabile

Erioderma pedicellatum

Cortinarius osloensis

Gloioxanthomyces vitellinus

Spongiforma squarepantsii

Porpolomopsis calyptriformis

Conservationists have listed the pink waxcap mushroom (*Hygrocybe calyptriformis*) as a threatened species. *Alan Rockefeller/ Mushroom Observer*

Conservation

Current threats to fungi include destruction of forests worldwide, **fragmentation** of habitat, changes in land use, pollution, climate change, and overharvesting of commercially attractive species. Sometimes it is hard to convince people that fungi need to be protected. They're called the hidden kingdom for a reason. Since so many types of fungi are microscopic, we can't see them without the aid of a microscope. Hundreds, even thousands, of fungi could be under our feet!

But mycologists are in a race against time. Every tree that is cut down in a rain forest destroys essential connections in the wood wide web. Other fungi are lost as land is developed and human civilization pushes in on nature.

Even as we destroy fungal habitats, mycologists are eagerly seeking more species of fungi for their potential uses in drugs, food, and bioremediation. Scientists understand the need to conserve our natural resources and put fungi to work in a variety of ways. One potential use is helping honeybees.

The widespread use of pesticides on agricultural crops has contributed to a steady decline in bee populations. This is a threat for people everywhere, as one out of every three bites of food you eat is made possible by those bee pollinators. Keeping bees alive is clearly in our best interest—especially for those who love to bite into a crisp apple, enjoy a smear of blueberry jelly on their toast, and can't summer without strawberries.

Honeybees face additional pressures. One of the biggest is a parasite called the Varroa mite. These mites suck the hemolymph—the insect equivalent of blood—from adults and developing larvae. By themselves, a big enough mite infestation can kill off a hive. But the mites can also carry viruses that kill bees. Commercial beekeepers usually treat their colonies with chemicals to stop the mites. But over time the mites adapt and the chemicals have no effect on them.

Can fungi help save the bees? Mycologist Paul Stamets thinks so. Many years ago, he noticed his honeybees visiting the mushroom patch he grew on a pile of woodchips in his yard. The bees flew back and forth between the mushrooms and the colony. They seemed to be feeding on something, so Paul took a closer look. The honeybees were drinking fungal extracts, tiny drops that formed on the very tips of the mycelium.

A few years passed. When a friend asked him how fungi could help save the honey-

A honeybee (*Apis mellifera*) visiting a bird cherry bloom (*Prunus padus*). *Ivar Leidus/ Wikimedia Commons*

FROM THE FUNGUS FILES:
Tinder fungus (*Fomes fomentarius*)

The amadou mushroom, *Fomes fomentarius*, grows thicker and thicker until it looks like a horse's hoof attached to the side of a tree. It's also called the tinder fungus because people have used it to help start their fires for more than 5,000 years!

People have also been using amadou mushrooms to treat inflammation for hundreds of years, so it makes sense to test whether this natural medicine might help other animals—including bees. Like other polypores, this fungus breaks down the lignin and cellulose in select trees, providing a habitat for birds and invertebrates.

Tinder fungus (*Fomes fomentarius*) found in Pennsylvania. *Hamilton/Mushroom Observer*

bees, Paul began to wonder, *What drew the honeybees to the mycelium extracts?* Paul had been researching polypore mushroom extracts and their potential to help people fight deadly viruses. That's when he had a eureka moment. If the mushroom extracts could help people fight off viruses, could they help the bees fight viruses too?

He gave several mushroom extracts to bees and discovered that it worked! Bees were living longer, and tests showed they carried fewer viruses. But he needed to test his theories on a bigger scale.

The almond tree bloom in San Joaquin Valley in California provided a strong testing group. Commercial beekeepers were hired to transport their honeybee colonies on trucks to pollinate the flowers on 800,000 trees. Paul gave the fungal extracts to bees in 532 hives for this field experiment. At the end, extracts from amadou mushrooms (*Fomes fomentarius*) and reishi mushrooms (*Ganoderma lucidum*) helped bees fend off mite-borne viruses. The potential of this new treatment is a promising, healthier way to help the bees.

Help Scientists Discover New Fungi

You don't have to be a scientist to discover a new fungus. Whether you call yourself a passionate amateur naturalist or a citizen scientist, you can help researchers by collecting and sharing your observations of the natural world.

One way to get involved is through Mushroom Observer (https://mushroom observer.org). Mushroom enthusiast Nathan Wilson started the site in 2006 as a place to display his fungus photos. Other people began sharing their photos and observations of mushrooms and lichens, creating a collaborative catalog of fungal diversity. By 2021 there were more than one million images from 9,000 contributors around the world. Add to that the notes about location and time of year the fungus was fruiting, and you've got a useful resource for professional mycologists as well as amateur naturalists.

Sometimes a photo can lead to a new discovery, or a rediscovery as one recent case shows. In 2013 Taylor Lockwood posted a photo of a fungus that looked like fingers in a white glove. Commonly called hazel gloves, *Hypocreopsis rhododendri* hadn't been recorded in the United States for a hundred years and was thought to be extinct.

If you really want to help scientists discover a new fungus, consider digging up a bit of soil from your yard. Researchers at the University of Oklahoma are searching for fungi that may help treat diseases. But they need to collect lots and lots of soil samples to find even one new fungus. It's hard for a scientist to travel all over the country collecting soil, so they are asking people to send them samples.

When a soil sample arrives, the scientists in the Natural Products Discovery Group spread the soil on the surface of a petri dish filled with a gel infused with stuff fungi like to eat: pulverized worms, sugars, ground up tomatoes, and "dirt tea." Once the fungi get growing, the scientists use DNA analysis to identify new species. Promising fungi are provided with their favorite food—Cheerios! Unlike you, the fungi sit down to their breakfast in a test tube.

After the fungi are established, the researchers begin looking for natural products the fungi produce and test them to see how they react to different diseases. They've already found some interesting results. One sample, sent from Alaska, contained a new fungus species that produced an unknown product. Even more exciting, it's a promising inhibitor of certain cancers!

Burial Shrouds and Coffins

When living organisms die, fungi get to work decomposing them. But did you know that bodies buried in a traditional coffin often take a decade or more to decompose? That's because morticians traditionally pump bodies full of formaldehyde to slow decomposition. Like other chemicals, formaldehyde pollutes groundwater and causes health problems, including cancer.

FROM THE FUNGUS FILES:
Agarikon (*Laricifomes officinalis*)

A mushroom that inhabits the forests in the northwestern United States and parts of Europe and Asia is *Laricifomes officinalis*, also known as agarikon. Almost 2,000 years before scientists discovered that fungi produce metabolites, a Greek physician, Pedanius Discorides, called this mushroom "the elixir of long life." Why? Because

this mushroom can live up to seventy-five years. Today, scientists know that it contains polyphenols and other metabolites that give it a strong immune system. Researchers hope to tap in to the antiviral compounds in agarikon to develop more medicines to address both known and unknown viruses.

Agarikon mushroom (*Laricifomes officinalis*) growing on a fir tree. *Steph Jarvis/ Mushroom Observer*

Some people choose cremation because they believe it's more natural and won't take up space in a cemetery. However, the Centers for Disease Control has found over 300 chemicals or residues in human tissue samples. During cremation, these chemicals and heavy metals are released into the atmosphere, adding to pollution.

Many states are passing laws to allow "green" or natural burials, which means the body is not treated with formaldehyde. Some states even allow burial without a coffin. But some people are still worried about all the chemicals in the bodies.

More than 10 years ago, artist Jae Rhim Lee began developing the Infinity Burial Suit. She describes it as a suit made "with a mix of mushroom spores and other microorganisms that help decompose the body, neutralize toxins, and transfer our bodies' nutrients to plants." In addition to this environmental role, she hopes to bring about a cultural shift about how we think about death and burials.

A company in the Netherlands created a coffin called a Living Cocoon, grown from fungal mycelium, to replace a standard wood or metal coffin.

Burial in a Living Cocoon or Infinity Burial Suit could eliminate the wastefulness of traditional burial and provide the

 **TRY THIS!**

Send a Soil Sample

Take the first step in joining the citizen science movement!

Here's what you need to do:

1. Ask an adult for permission to go to whatsinyourbackyard.org and click the "Participate" button. You'll need to fill out a form giving your name, email address, and mailing address. The program will send you a free soil-collection kit.

2. When the kit arrives in the mail, choose a spot in your yard that people don't walk through often. Areas under trees or bushes, especially where leaves fall, are ideal. Scoop up some soil from this area, but not deeper than you can poke a finger into the ground.

3. Pack up your kit and prepare to ship it back to the program. If you're under 18 years old, ask a parent or guardian to sign the collection form so your sample can be used.

4. When your sample arrives at the University of Oklahoma, they will test it and document their discoveries on a website where you can see photos of fungi from your sample and read about what was "unearthed." But try to be patient. It can take several months to grow the fungi, run the tests, and post updates about them.

right fungi to begin breaking down the human body and the chemicals it contains. Decomposition would take only two to three years instead of more than a decade.

Make Paper Out of Fungi

Making paper from mushrooms is similar to making paper from plants. The biggest difference is that mushroom paper is more fibrous and better for crafts than for writing.

Mushrooms that get tough and leathery like this polypore can be used to make paper. *Sue Heavenrich/Author photo*

MATERIALS

- Mushrooms (polypore mushrooms work better than soft, fleshy mushrooms)
- Bucket
- Frame or embroidery hoop
- Wire, plastic screen, or netting fabric
- Stapler
- Large dishpan or tub
- Newspapers, rags, towels, old sheeting, old blanket, heavy brown paper, or paper towels
- Blender you don't use for food
- Knife
- Construction paper and other paper scraps
- Sponges
- A board and some books to serve as a weight

1. Soak the mushrooms in a bucket. Hard mushrooms, such as conks, may need to soak for a week or more. Change the water every day. Fleshy mushrooms can soak overnight.

2. Make a screen. An old picture frame or embroidery hoop from a second-hand store is perfect. Screen can be wire (like window screen) or plastic needlepoint screen, or even nylon netting. Staple it to the frame or fix it into an embroidery hoop.

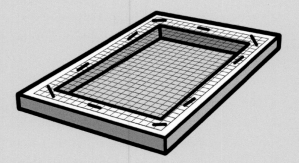

3. Fill the dishpan or tub with a few inches of water.

4. Lay down a layer of towels and newspapers on a table or other flat surface.

5. Tear or chop up the softened mushrooms into small pieces, then add them to the blender and puree them, being sure to blend in batches if need be, depending on the size of the blender used. If you are using soft, fleshy mushrooms, add paper strips to the blender. The paper will add fiber to your mushroom stock. You want to blend to a puree. Tough mushrooms will need to be blended a bit at a time so you don't burn out the blender.

6. Pour the mushroom slurry into the dishpan—slowly. The slurry should float in a layer on the water. Break up any mushroom bits with your fingers. If you can see through it, add more mushroom mix.

7. Remove fibers from the slurry. Dip the frame, screen-side up, into the fibers, at an angle. Level it underneath the slurry and lift it up. Gently shake to smooth mushroom fibers over the screen. You can dip again if you need to catch more fibers. Hold the screen at the edge of the tub and let excess water drain back into the tub.

8. Couching (KOO-ching) is the term for getting the paper off the screen. Set the screen next to the towels. Then quickly flip it over so the paper side is on the stack of newspapers and towels. Use a sponge to remove excess water from the screen. Then lift screen off the paper. If the mushroom paper sticks to the screen, use the sponge to rewet the paper.

9. Put another towel or layer of newspapers over your paper. Then lay a weight on top to keep it flat while drying. A board with books or stones works well. Let dry for a few hours.

Make Compost in a Soda Bottle

Gardeners harness the work of fungi and other decomposers to turn leaves and vegetable scraps into compost, a nutrient-rich food for plants. Compost bins take up a lot of space, but you can make a mini-composter out of an old soda bottle. And when your compost is ready, you can plant a flower in it!

MATERIALS

- 🍄 1 empty 2-liter soda bottle
- 🍄 Scissors
- 🍄 Nail
- 🍄 Flat dish to hold the soda bottle such as a take-out container
- 🍄 Soil from outside (not potting soil)
- 🍄 Shredded newspaper, dead leaves
- 🍄 Spray bottle
- 🍄 Organic matter such as grass clippings, vegetable scraps, fruit peelings, egg shells, and used coffee grounds or tea bags
- 🍄 Marker
- 🍄 Washcloth
- 🍄 Your FUNgus Journal
- 🍄 Ruler or measuring tape

1. Rinse out the bottle to make sure there's no sugary stuff that will attract ants. Then peel off the label.

2. Cut off the top of the bottle above the shoulder.

3. Use a nail to make holes in the bottom and sides of the bottle.

4. Stand your bottle on the dish or plastic tray. Scoop in about an inch of dirt from outside. Add about an inch of shredded newspaper and old leaves. Spray your compost starter with enough water to make it damp, but not soaked.

5. Add organic matter—about the same amount as your leaves and paper. Spritz with water.

6. Add another layer of soil, leaves, and paper, and another layer of organic matter. Top it off with some soil and leaves and grass. Spritz again.

7. Draw a line to mark the starting level of your compost and put it in the sun. Cover the top with a washcloth.

8. Create a "Compost" page in your journal. Write down the date and draw a picture to show how you made your compost layers. Measure how tall your compost pile is inside the bottle. Once a week, measure and take notes on your compost. Spritz it with water to maintain a fungus-friendly environment. Eventually, you should end up with rich soil, perfect for planting a seed.

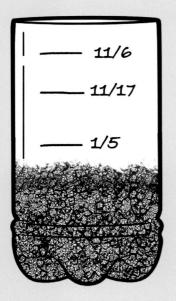

11/6

11/17

1/5

Glossary

acid: a substance with sour taste that changes blue litmus paper to red

amino acid: Small molecules that are the building blocks of proteins

base: a substance that reacts with acid to form a salt and turns red litmus paper to blue

binomial nomenclature: The system of giving two names, the genus and species, to each organism

biocontrol: A method of controlling pests and disease by using other organisms

biome: A large, naturally occurring community of plants and animals occupying a major habitat, for example a forest

budding: The type of reproduction found in yeasts, in which a new individual develops by cell division and pinches off

caps: The wide, top parts of mushroom fruiting bodies that sit atop stalks

chitin: A complex carbohydrate found in the cell walls of fungi and the exoskeletons of arthropods

compound: A substance formed when two or more chemical elements are chemically bonded together

decomposer: An organism that feeds on and breaks down dead or decaying plants or animals, and returns nutrients to the ecosystem

ecosystem: A community of living organisms and the physical environment in which they interact

endangered: A species threatened by extinction

entomopathogenic: Fungi that infect insects and eventually kill them

enzyme: A biological catalyst, usually a protein, that speeds up a chemical reaction

fermentation: The process of breaking down complex molecules into simpler ones, producing alcohol and carbon dioxide

flagellum: a thin, hairlike structure that allows a cell to move

forensic: Analysis of evidence, such as spores and pollen, to help solve a crime

fragmentation: The process of being broken into smaller pieces

fruiting body: A general term for the fungal structures that contain spores, commonly called the mushroom

gills: Paper-thin ribs beneath the caps of some mushroom species that serve as a means of spore dispersal

habitat: The natural home or environment of an organism

heterotroph: An organism that does not have the ability to produce its own food and must get nutrition from another source

hyphae: Branching threadlike structures that make up the mycelium of a fungus

invasive: An introduced organism that becomes overpopulated and causes harm to its new environment

lichen: A symbiotic community made up of one or more fungus species plus an alga and/or cyanobacterium

Metabolic product: a compound produced by the cells of a fungus

metabolite: An intermediate or end product of the chemical reactions that take place in living cells

mitosis: A process in which one cell divides into two identical cells, each containing the same parts and genetic code as the parent cell

mold: A fungus that grows in the form of filaments called hyphae

molecule: The smallest part of a material that has all the physical and chemical properties of that material

mushroom: The conspicuous above-ground fruiting body of certain fungi

mutualism: A symbiotic association between two or more species in which each species benefits

mycelium: The mass of branching and interwoven hyphae that forms the body of the fungus

mycology: The study of fungi

mycoremediation: A kind of biological remediation in which fungi are used to decontaminate the environment

mycorrhizal: A mutual symbiotic relationship that forms between a fungus and a plant

mycotroph: A plant that gets its nutrients from fungi

nutrient: Substances an organism needs for energy, building materials, and metabolism

palynomorphs: Pollen grains and spores

parasite: An organism that lives on or in a host organism, often causing it harm

pathogen: An organism that causes disease to its host

photosynthesis: a process in which green plants use energy from the sun to turn carbon dioxide and water into food

phylum: The primary subdivision of a kingdom

saprotroph: An organism that feeds on dead plants, animals, or other organisms

spore: A reproductive cell adapted for dispersal and capable of developing into a new individual

stalk: The stemlike part of a mushroom that supports the cap

symbiosis: Two or more species living in a close and long-term relationship

truffle: The underground fruiting body of certain fungi

Online Resources

Websites

Backyard Fungi
www.backyardnature.net/f/2fungi.htm

Fun with Fungi
https://herbarium.usu.edu/fun-with-fungi

Mushroom Observer
https://mushroomobserver.org

North American Mycological Association
https://namyco.org

The University of Oklahoma Citizen Science Soil Collection Program
https://whatsinyourbackyard.org

International Union for Conservation of Nature's Red List
www.iucnredlist.org

State of the World's Plants and Fungi, Royal Botanic Gardens, Kew
www.kew.org/science/state-of-the-worlds-plants-and-fungi

Videos

Visit Hawk Meadow Mushroom Farm
www.woodlanders.com/blog/2017/3/20/episode-4-woodland-mushroom-cultivation

A Tour of Warwick Mushroom Farm
https://vimeo.com/446284078

How Ecovative Design Turns Mycelium into Biodegradable Packaging
https://youtu.be/i7FCkK44UcY

"Spalted Wood" Series with Artist Mark Lindquist and Artist/Scientist Dr. Sara Robinson
www.northernspalting.com/documentary-on-spalted-wood/

"How to Bundle Dye at Home with Food Waste"
https://youtu.be/9G64jioXlnI.

Teacher's Guide

— — — — —

The activities and information in this book can be used with a wide range of ages, either in the classroom or for independent study. If you'd like to explore further, consider some of the ideas listed here.

❑ Create a word search or crossword puzzle using names of fungi or words from the glossary.

❑ Ask each student to research a different species that lives in your area and create a local fungus guide. Vote on one as the "class fungus" and make a poster for the classroom door.

❑ Celebrate fungi on National Mushroom Day (October 15). Have students research any threatened or endangered fungi in your area and come up with ways to protect them.

❑ Go on a mycelium search around the schoolyard or local park. Look for white mycelium threads on rotten logs (may be under the bark) and under old leaf piles.

❑ If you have a nature center or fungi-rich park, go on a fungus scavenger hunt. Create a list or bingo card that asks students to look for different colors, different textures, different shapes, and different substrates.

❑ Have students explore careers for a mycologist. Here's a few: museum curator, park naturalist, crime scene investigator, pharmaceutical researcher, or any role in the fields of pollution control and remediation or agriculture.

❑ Visit a cemetery and have students compare the types of lichens growing on gravestones and memorial markers. Do different kinds of lichens grow on different kinds of stones?

❑ Buy a mushroom-growing kit and have students keep an observation journal as the mushrooms grow. When the mushrooms are ready, use them to top a pizza, add to a salad, or stir-fry.

❑ Discuss the following questions:

What important roles do fungi play in the ecosystem?
What would happen if you removed them?
How do fungi help humans?
Why is it important to protect fungi?

❑ Research one of these scientists further:

- Carl Linnaeus
- Heinrich Anton de Bary
- Alexander Fleming
- Howard Florey
- Beatrix Potter (not well-known as a mycologist!)

Notes

Chapter 2: Sorting Out the Fungi

"I find things by going out": Kathie Hodge, phone interview by author Sue Heavenrich, September 29, 2020.

Chapter 4: Fungi as Food

"Shiitake mushrooms are sapwood feeders": Steve Sierigk, phone interview by author Sue Heavenrich, March 3, 2021; and *Woodlanders*, episode 4, "Woodland Mushroom Cultivation," directed by Costa Boutsikaris, aired March 2017, www.woodlanders.com/blog/2017/3/20/episode-4-woodland-mushroom-cultivation.

Chapter 6: The Fungal Pharmacy

"I did not invent penicillin": Siang Yong Tan and Yvonne Tatsumura, "Alexander Fleming (1881–1955): Discoverer of penicillin," *Singapore Medical Journal* 56 (2015): 366–367, https://www.ncbi.nlm.nih.gov/pmc/articles/PMC4520913.

Chapter 7: Putting Fungi to Work

"It involves aspects of botany": Patricia E. Wiltshire, *The Nature of Life and Death: Every Body Leaves a Trace* (New York: Putnam, 2019).

"laid out templates and bricks": David Benjamin, email correspondence with author Alisha Gabriel, May 5, 2021.

Chapter 8: The Future of Fungi

"with a mix of mushroom spores": Jae Rhim Lee, "How the Mushroom Death Suit Will Change the Way We Die," Ted Fellows blog, April 13, 2016, https://fellowsblog.ted.com/how-the-mushroom-death-suit-will-change-the-way-we-die-a52f486dc816.

Bibliography

* Denotes titles suitable for young readers.

Books

Antonelli, Alexandre, ed. *State of the World's Plants and Fungi, 2020*. Royal Botanic Gardens, Kew, 2020. www.kew.org /science/state-of-the-worlds-plants-and-fungi.

*Billups, Carla, and Dawn Cusick. *It's a Fungus Among Us: The Good, the Bad & the Downright Scary*. Mission Viejo, CA: Moondance Press/Quarto Publishing, 2017.

*Boddy, Lynne. *Humongous Fungus*. New York: DK Children, 2021.

*Gravel, Elise. *The Mushroom Fan Club*. Montreal: Drawn and Quarterly, 2018.

*Koch, Melissa. *Forest Talk: How Trees Communicate*. Minneapolis, MN: Twenty-First Century Books, 2019

Lax, Eric. *The Mold in Dr Florey's Coat: the Story of the Penicillin Miracle*. Henry Holt & Co., 2004.

Sheldrake, Merlin. *Entangled Life: How Fungi Make Our Worlds, Change Our Minds and Shape Our Futures*. New York: Random House, 2020.

Wiltshire, Patricia E. *The Nature of Life and Death: Every Body Leaves a Trace*. New York: G. P. Putnam's Sons, 2019.

Field Guides

*DK. *Mushrooms: How to Identify and Gather Wild Mushrooms and Other Fungi*. New York: DK, 2013.

*McKnight, Karl B., et al. *Peterson Field Guide to Mushrooms of North America*. Boston: Houghton Mifflin Harcourt, 2021.

*National Audubon Society. *National Audubon Society Field Guide to North American Mushrooms*. New York: Knopf, 1981.

*Roberts, Peter, and Shelley Evans. *The Book of Fungi: A Life-Size Guide to Six Hundred Species from Around the World*. Chicago: University of Chicago Press, 2011.

Index

Note: Page numbers in *italics* refer to photographs and illustrations.

absorbency, 74
Adidas, 87
agarikon (*Laricifomes officinalis*), 98, *98*
aggregates, 32
algae, 29, 40, 42
amadou mushrooms (*Fomes fomentarius*), *viii*, 97, *97*
amateur naturalists, 97–98
amatoxin, 52
ambrosia beetles, 36
amino acids, 8
amoebas, 29
amphibian chytrid fungus (*Batrachochytrium dendrobatidis*), 26, *26*
anatomy, 6, 8
animals, 2–3, 5, 35–36
antibiotics, 70–72, 75–76

architecture, 88–89
Aristotle, 2
ascocarps, 16, 20
Ascomycota (phylum), 16, 20
ascus and asci, 20, 23, *23*
Aspergillus fungi, 2, 11, 51

Baker's yeast (*Saccharomyces cerevisiae*), 8, 50, *50*
bark beetles, 58
basidia, 23
Basidiomycota (phylum), 23–24, 26
Beauveria bassiana fungus, 85–86, *85*
beefsteak fungus (*Fistulina hepatica*), 53
Benjamin, David, 89
binomial nomenclature, 6
biocontrol sprays, 85
bioluminescent mushroom (*Mycena chlorophos*), 24, *24*
biomes, 42

biopesticides, 85–86
bioremediation, 94, 96
bird's nest fungi, 24
black truffles (*Tuber mealosporum*), 49, *49*
Blastomyces dermatitidis, 63, 65
blight fungus (*Alternaria solani*), 61
bolete mushrooms, *23*, 24
Borel, Jean-François, 75
bracket fungi, 24
brain mushroom (*Gyromitra esculenta*), 52, *52*
budding, 10
bundle dyeing, 90–91
button mushrooms (*Agaricus bisporus*), 23, *44*, 46

cancer, 77–78
carbohydrates, 36–37
caterpillar fungus (*Ophiocordyceps sinensis*), 76, *76*

cellulose, 5, 29, 33, 35
Centers for Disease Control, 99
Chain, Ernst, 72
charcoal-loving elf cup (*Geopyxis carbonaria*), 32, *32*
cheese, 51
Chicken of the Woods, 24
Chinese medicine, 76–77
chitin, 5, 16, 23, 26, 28, 29, 33
chlorophyll, 2
chocolate, 50–51
cholesterol, 72–73
Chytridiomycota (phylum), 26
class, 16, *16*
classification, 2–3, 5–6, 15–16, 17
club fungi. *see* Basidiomycota (phylum)
Coccidioides fungus, 63
compactin, 73
compost, 46–47, 87, 102–103
compounds, 29
conservation, 96–99
coral fungus (*Clavaria zollingeri*), 10, *10*
corn, 61
corn mushroom. *see* huitlacoche (corn mushroom)
Cortinarius semisanguineus, 89, *89*
cremation, 99
cremini mushrooms, 46. *see also* button mushrooms (*Agaricus bisporus*)
crops, 58–59, 63
crustose lichens, *42*, 42–43
cup fungi, 20, 32

cyanobacteria, 40
cyclosporine, 75–76

de Bary, Heinrich Anton, 40
death and burials, 98–99
death cap mushroom (*Amanita phalloides*), 23, 52–53
decomposers, viii, 2–3, 33, 98–99
deforestation, 96
destroying angel mushrooms (*Amanita bisporigera*), 52–53, *53*
Dickinson, Emily, 40
Discorides, Pedanius, 98
disease, 69–74
DNA analysis, 5, 16–17, 73, 82, 85, 98
Douglas fir trees, 36–37
drug testing, 73–76
Duchesne, Ernest A. C., 70
Dutch elm disease (*Ophiostoma ulmi*), 58–59
dyes, 89–91, *89*

earthstars, 24
ecosystem, 9
ecosystem pioneers, 43
Ecovative Design, 86–88
edible mushrooms, 23, 51–53
emerald ash borer beetles, *85*, 86
endangered, ix, 95
Endo, Akira, 73
entomopathogenic fungi, 65–66, 85, 86
 Entomophaga maimaiga fungus, 86
 Entomophthora muscae, 65

environment, 1–2, 32–33
environmental sequencing, 17
enzymes, 8, 33, 84–85
ergot fungus (*Claviceps purpurea*), 58, *58*
eukaryotic organisms, 5

family, 16, *16*
farming, 46–49
fermentation, 45, 50–51
filamentous lichens, 43
Fire Mediation Action Coalition, 94
flagellum, 26
Fleming, Sir Alexander, 70, *70*, 72–73
Florey, Howard, 72
fly agaric (*Amanita muscaria*), *14. see also* yellow fly agaric (*Amanita muscaria* var. *formosa*)
foliose lichens, 43
food, 45–46, 49–51, 60
Food and Drug Administration (FDA), 73–74, 76, 77
food chain, 33, 35
food for animals, 35–36
foraging, 51–54
forensic ecology, 82, 84
formaldehyde, 98
Frey, Hans Peter, 75
frogs, 26, *26*
fruiting bodies, 3, 9, 32, 47, 49,96. *see also* ascocarps
 anatomy and, 6, 8
 as food, 35

mushrooms as, viii
  of phylum Ascomycota, 16, 20
  of phylum Basidiomycota, 23–24
  spores and, 2
fungicide, 62
fungology. *see* mycology and mycologists
fungus and fungi, *80*

galls, 61
genus, 6, 16, *16*
Geological Survey of Canada, 33
ghost plants (*Monotropa uniflora*), 40
giant puffball mushroom (*Calvatia gigantea*), *11*
gills, 23–24
golden chanterelle (*Catharellus formosus*), *78*
grass, 34
gray mold, *56*, 61
green burials, 99
green elf cup fungus (*Chlorociboria aeruginascens*), 88, *88*
green lacewing larvae, 42, *42*
gyromitrin, 52

habitat loss, ix, 96
haiku, 85
hallucinogenic mushrooms (*Psilocybe semilanceata*), 78–79, *79*
Hat Thrower fungus (*Pilobolus crystallinus*), 28, *28*
Hawk Meadow Farm, 47

hazel glove fungus (*Hypocreopsis rhododendri*), 98
hemolymph, 96
herbicides, 86
Herrick, Richard, 75
Herrick, Ronald, 75
heterotrophs, 33
high-density lipoprotein (HDL) cholesterol, 72–73
Hodge, Kathie T., 17, *17*, 20, 23
honeybees (*Apis mellifera*), 96–97, *96*
huitlacoche (corn mushroom), 60–61
"humongous fungus" (*Armillaria ostoyae*), 2–3
Hy-Fi Tower, 88–89, *88*
hyphae, 2, 8–9, *9*, 29, 31–33, 43

immunosuppressants, 75–76
infections, 63
Infinity Burial Suit, 99
insects, 35–36, 65–66, *66*
invasive fungi, 58
Irish potato famine, 63

jack-o-lantern fungus (*Omphalotus olearius*), *ix*
jelly ear fungus (*Auricularia auricula-judae*), 6, *6*

Kennett Square, Pennsylvania, 53
kingdom, 2–3, *16*
kudzu plants, 86

lattice stinkhorn mushroom (*Clathrus ruber*), *11*
laundry detergent, 84–85
leafcutter ants, 36, *36*
Lee, Jae Rhim, 99
lentinan, 77
lichens, viii, 25, *30*, 31, 40–43, *40*, 79, 98
lignin, 33, 35, 84, 87, 97
Linnaeus, Carl, 6, 15
Lion's mane mushrooms (*Hericium erinaceus*), 46, 75, *75*
lipoproteins, 72–73
litmus paper and dye, 42
Living Cocoon coffin, 99
lobster mushroom (*Hypomyces lactifluorum*), 66, *66*
Locard, Edmond, 82
Locard's exchange principle, 82
Lockwood, Taylor, 98
Loren, Corentin, 33
low-density lipoprotein (LDL) cholesterol, 72–73
Lymantria dispar caterpillar, 86
lysine, 61
lysozyme, 70

marine fungi, 77
medicine. *see* antibiotics; Chinese medicine
metabolic products, 73
metabolites, 73, 75, 77
Micheli, Pier Antonio, 2, *3*, 11
microbiomes, 42

microclimate, 48
Microsporidia (phylum), 28
milk, 63
mitosis, 10
mold, viii, 8–9, 50–51, *56*, 70, 83
molecules, 5
mordant, 89
morel mushrooms (*Morchella esculenta*), 20, 35, 51–52, *52*
Mucoromycota (phylum), 26, 28
mummy berry fungus, 63
mushroom farming, 46–49
Mushroom Festival (Kennett Square, Pennsylvania), 53
Mushroom Observer, 97
mushrooms
    commercial farming of, 46–47
    as food, 35–36, 45–46
mutualism, 40
mycelium, *9*
    defined, 8
    honeybees and, 96–97
    mushroom farming and, 46–48
    packing material and, 86–88
    plants and insects and, 35–36
    soil and, 31–32
mycelium bricks, 88–89, *88*
Mycena leaiana var. *australis*, *x*
myco-leather, 87
mycology and mycologists, 1–3, 15–16, 17, 96
mycoparasites, 86

mycoremediation, 94
mycorrhizal fungi, 49
mycorrhizal network, 36–37, *37*, 86
MycoStix, 89
mycotrophs, 37, 40
Myrothecium verrucaria fungus, 86

nail infections, 63
Natural Products Discovery Group (University of Oklahoma), 98
Nobel Prize, 72
Northern Regional Research Laboratory (NRRL), 72
nutrients, viii
nutrition, 45

octopus stinkhorn (*Clathrus archeri*), *ix*
oomycetes (water molds), 28–29
orange peel fungus (*Aleuria aurantia*), 20, *20*
order, 16, *16*
organ transplants, 75–76
oyster mushrooms (*Pleurotus ostreatus*), 46, 84, *84*, *92*, 94

packing material, 86–87, *86*
palynomorphs, 82, 84
papermaking, 100–101
parasites, 28, 66
parasitic fungus (*Nosema ceranae*), 28
Pasteur, Louis, 50
pathogens, 26

penicillin, 70, 72
Penicillium (genus), 16
Penicillium citrinum, 73, *73*
Penicillium glaucum, 70
Penicillium roqueforti, 51
Penicillium rubens, 9, *72*
pesticides, 93–94. *see also* biopesticides
photosynthesis, 2, 33, 40
phylum, 16, *16*, 20, 23
    Ascomycota, 16, 20, 23
    Basidiomycota, 23–24, 26
    Chytridiomycota, 26
    Microsporidia, 28
    Mucoromycota, 26, 28
Phytophthora infestans, 63
Pink Indian Pipes, *40*
pink waxcap mushroom (*Hygrocybe calyptriformis*), *95*
plants, 2–3, 5, 28, 32–33, 36–37, 57–63
pollutants and contaminants, 93–94
polyphenols, 98
polypore mushrooms, 89, 97, *100*
polysaccharide-K (PSK), 77
portobello mushrooms, 46. *see also* button mushrooms (*Agaricus bisporus*)
postage stamps, 71, *71*
potatoes, 61
powdery mildew fungus, 61, *61*, 63
proteases, 84
psilocybin, 78–79
puffballs, 24, 35

Rainbird, Robert, 33
Raistrick, Harold, 70
red fly agaric (*Amanita muscaria*), 53
reishi mushrooms (*Ganoderma lucidum*), 77, *77*, 97
Rice, Miriam C., 89
ringworm, 63
rust fungi, 59, *59*

sac fungi. *see* Ascomycota (phylum)
Salem witch trials, 58
saprobes, 24, *24*
saprotrophs, 33
scarlet caterpillar club fungus (*Cordyceps militaris*), 20, 65–66, *65*
Schol-Schwarz, Marie Beatrice (Bea), 58
Sheldrake, Merlin, 42
shelf fungi, 24
shiitake mushrooms (*Lentinula edodes*), 46–48, *47*, 77
Sierigk, Anna, 48
Sierigk, Steve, 47–48
Simard, Dr. Suzanne, 37
slime molds, 29
smut fungus (*Ustilago maydis*), 60, 61, *61*
soil, 31–33, 68, 72–73, 75, 82, 94, 98–99
sourdough yeast (*Saccharomyces exiguus*), 50
soy sauce, 51
spalted wood, 87–88, *87*
spawn, 46–47
species, 6, 15–16, *16*

Spongiforma squarepantsii, 6, 11
spores
    ascomycetes and, 20
    basidia and, 23–24
    Coccidioides fungus and, 63
    discovery of, 2
    Hat Thrower fungus and, 28
    molds and fruiting bodies and, 8–10
    plants and, 58–59
    spore prints and, 21, 52
    wildfires and, 32
squamulose lichens, 43
stalks, 6
Stamets, Paul, 96–97
Stan Smith Mylo sneakers (Adidas), 87, *87*
Staphylococcus bacteria, 70
state fungus, 78
statins, 72–73
stinkhorns, 24, 26
substrate, 46
symbiosis and symbiotic relationships, 36, 40

taxonomy and taxonomists, 6, 17
termites, 35–36
Termitomyces, 35
Texas star mushroom (*Choriaster geaster*), *11*
The Living company, 88–89
thrush, 63
tinder fungus. *see* amadou mushrooms (*Fomes fomentarius*)

Tolypocladium inflatum gams, 75
tomatoes, 61
toxins, 52–53
Trichoderma fungi, 86
triterpenoids, 77
truffles, 20, 23, 35, 49–50. *see also* black truffles (*Tuber mealosporum*); white truffles (*Tuber magnatum*)
turkey tail mushrooms (*Trametes versicolor*), 35, *35*, 77

University of Oklahoma, 98–99
uses of fungi, 81–89

valley fever, 63
varieties of fungi, viii–ix
Varroa mites, 96–97

Warwick Mushroom Farms, 46–47
water molds. *see* oomycetes (water molds)
wattles, 94
Weston, Dillon, 59
wheat and grains, 58–59
White, David J. G., 76
white rot fungi, 33
white truffles (*Tuber magnatum*), 49–50
Whittaker, Robert, 2–3
wildfires, 32, 94
wildflowers, 36–37
Wilson, Nathan, 97
Wiltshire, Patricia, 82, 84
wood wide web, 37, *37*, 96

woodworking, 87–88

wych elm (*Ulmus glabra*), 58

yeasts, 10, 40, 50–51, 63. *see also* baker's
   yeast (*Saccharomyces cerevisiae*);
   sourdough yeast (*Saccharomyces exiguus*)

yellow fly agaric (*Amanita muscaria* var.
   formosa), 8. *see also* fly agaric (*Amanita
   muscaria*)

Young Architects Program competition, 88

zombifying fungi, 65–67